SIR THOMAS MORE

SIR THOMAS MORE
From an engraving by F. Bartolozzi after an original drawing
by Hans Holbein

# SIR
# THOMAS MORE

## LESLIE PAUL

**BOOKS FOR LIBRARIES PRESS**
FREEPORT, NEW YORK

First Published 1953

Reprinted 1970 by arrangement with Leslie Paul and his
literary agents, Collins-Knowlton-Wing, Inc.

INTERNATIONAL STANDARD BOOK NUMBER:
0-8369-5502-1

LIBRARY OF CONGRESS CATALOG CARD NUMBER:
75-128882

PRINTED IN THE UNITED STATES OF AMERICA

Dedicated

to the young scholars

PAUL and CYNTHIA

# CONTENTS

# ILLUSTRATIONS

# ACKNOWLEDGEMENTS

I wish to acknowledge my gratitude to Messrs. Burns Oates and Washbourne for permission to quote from Father Bridgett's *Life and Writings of Blessed Thomas More*, to Messrs. A. and C. Black for permission to quote from Karl Kautsky's *Thomas More and his Utopia* and A. R. Hope-Moncrieff's *A Book about Schools*, and to Messrs. Longmans Green for permission to use F. M. Nichols's translations of Erasmus's Epistles, published in the *Epistles of Erasmus*, Vols. I and II, 1901–4. I am glad to thank Miss H. J. Nutter and Mr. A. S. Bennell for help in checking the manuscripts and the proofs.

Acknowledgements are also due to the Director of the National Portrait Gallery for permission to reproduce the portraits of Henry VIII and John Fisher; to the Librarian, Chelsea Public Library, for permission to reproduce the Bartolozzi engraving of Sir Thomas More; to the Executors of the late Lord St. Oswald for permission to reproduce a detail from the Locky copy of the Holbein family group.

# CHAPTER ONE

# 'DISCORD AND DISSENSION'

There are resemblances between the sixteenth century and our own. England upon the accession of Henry VIII could look back, like the England of Edward VII, upon a long period of peace. The coffers were full, the threat of the barbarian Turk hardly more real than the yellow peril to the government of Mr. Asquith, and Christendom so secure that its disappearance could not be imagined. In the first decade of the twentieth century a world order of a sort seemed also to be established. It was possible to travel without passport, or other inquisition, throughout most of Europe, and with rather more ease than Erasmus had done on the nag presented to him by the Rector of Hackney, and the gold coin of our fathers was its own guarantor, and needed no world bank. The liberal order was not simply a commercial one; there was a free intellectual currency too, and science and philosophy, art and literature, enjoyed a liberty and prestige before which even governments bowed. The stability of the world was rooted in a triumphant past. The nineteenth century had witnessed the most marvellous scientific advances, which had produced a rising standard of living for all classes, an increase in man's mastery over nature, and an impressive conquest of disease and suffering. It was not supposed that they would come to an end—and if they did not, if they continued to soar, what then? What limits could be put to the victories of the spirit? How could man avoid bringing most of the causes of personal misery and social unrest to an end? There was a new wind blowing, exhilarating the young

men, bringing them to feel that at last mankind was on the
verge of shedding its follies and shaping human institutions in
the light of reason, and with the energy born of a new moral
fervour.

It was with boundless confidence that the brilliant young
men of the turn of the century, Bernard Shaw, Oscar Wilde,
H. G. Wells, Bertrand Russell, tilted at contemporary follies,
tumbled over the idols, lashed out at the timidities and greed
of the *bourgeoisie*, or the corruptions of governments and all
other established institutions. There was hardly a young man
of mettle to be found who was not ready, at a moment's notice,
to set right what was wrong with the world, and the better
educated he was, the more gently raised, the more eager, often
enough, to begin the construction of the new world on his first
Saturday down from the 'varsity.

Thomas More and Erasmus, and the whole company of
humanists, Colet, Grocyn, Linacre, Fisher and so forth, exer-
cising their wits over the vanities of princes, over the corruptions of the papacy and the church, satirizing the idleness of
monks and wandering friars, scornful of superstitions, contemptuous of the insanity of war, were not unlike the intellectuals of our century, and they were just as ready to produce
policies for universal peace, new systems of education, or blue
prints for a new society. Their Renaissance has points of similarity with the Victorian age too. The introduction of printing
to England in 1471 brought about a ferment like that engineered
by the universal education act of 1870. Is it fanciful to assert
that the birth of the popular press in our time has had an effect
resembling the increasing currency of translations of the Bible
in the sixteenth century? Would to God, one must say, with as
noble a consequence for English prose! The discovery of
America in 1492, and of the Cape route to the East Indies in
1497, opened men's eyes to the vastness of their contemporary
world just as effectively as Darwin's theories enlarged for us
our own historical and biological past. The new learning which

the Italian Renaissance spread abroad watered the deserts of
medieval theology and a new humanism flowered. The
Christian austerities were softened by the *humanitas* of classical
Greece. It was a more profound movement, but was it so unlike the religion of humanity which Comte distilled from a
similar ferment? At the dawn of the earlier century the era of
the poet-statesman and the scholar-prince seemed to be at
hand; and the clear intellectual light shed abroad by the new
thinkers promised to make bright the way which a reformed
Church might take to bring men to a golden age. The disap-
pointments ahead of More's age could no more be foreseen
than those which lay in ambush for Comte's. In our time, out
of the moral and intellectual ferments of a century, have sprung
the humourless fanaticisms of Fascism and Communism, and
their global wars and persecutions. Just so the golden age hoped
for by the new humanism issued in the militant and anti-intel-
lectual protestantism of Luther, the Inquisition of Loyola, and
the century of religious wars in which medieval Christian unity
was finally defended by no one. The age of reform, then as
now, gave way to an era of irreconcilable ideologies.

The overwhelming problem which has faced many a contemporary European has been how far he shall permit his
government to control his soul; we have had to fight out this
business all over again after it had been believed settled once
and for all in the nineteenth century; just so the dilemma (of
the division of loyalty between Church and State) the Middle
Ages had once brilliantly solved, brought Thomas More to his
martyrdom. There is good reason therefore to turn back to the
sixteenth century and look upon the struggle between the conscience of man and the power of the secular order revealed
there, for the light it throws upon moral decisions we, too,
must make.

However, it is dangerous to press historical analogies too far.
What must not be obscured is the unlikeness of the sixteenth
century to our own. England was then a puny province of

Christendom, not the heart of a mighty world empire. Her population was less than the population of Greater London to-day: in communications she was poor, in manufactures inferior to the Netherlands, in the civilized arts far behind Italy. Unity and nationhood were new things, slowly emerging after the devastating Wars of the Roses. It was Henry VII, the first of the Tudors, who in the boyhood of Thomas More established the civil truce which healed the wounds of the country, re-stored firm government and allowed treasure to be amassed. It was indeed to the exertions of his dull and miserly father that Henry VIII owed the Renaissance splendour of his reign; it was through those same exertions that he found awaiting him a young, self-conscious nation searching for a king who would glorify and enrich it. It was an England at its beginnings, not at its zenith, over which he ruled, and yet which first in his reign began impudently to seek to dominate Europe by the exercise of the balance of power, a policy which brought its advocate, Wolsey, to ruin.

It is a revelation of the position of the Church in England at the opening of the sixteenth century that Wolsey, Henry VIII's Lord Chancellor, was as great and glorious a prince as Henry himself—as a cardinal of the Church who was at the same time head of his country's government was bound to be. He was also the last of the line of ecclesiastical statesmen. In the late fifteenth century the Church, though far from popular, was uniquely entrenched, well cushioned with temporal privi-leges, and without a real challenge in the spiritual sphere. It was the owner of manors and estates without end, with com-mand over the livings of parish priests, and possessed of collec-tive institutions to which the only parallel to-day would be the armed forces of a nation. And this spiritual army had its bar-racks, depots, training establishments and transit camps. It was an institution which had cultivated and preserved the civilized arts, sweetened and enlightened society, and, since Saxon days, laboured to lift the nation out of barbarism. From it, as a matter of course, princes recruited their civil servants and diplomats, and the universities their teachers. But it was also like an army which had too long enjoyed the comfort of peace-time stations and had forgotten that there were other duties than formal or ceremonial parades.

The loyalty of this highly organized international institution to Rome, the source of Christian light and teaching, was naturally an acceptable thing until the rise of strong national feelings called into question the ecclesiastical discipline, the separate courts, the 'foreign' allegiance, and converted these prerogatives of the Church into obstacles to the supremacy of a temporal prince. This new national spirit in More's day was closely connected with the rise of an aspiring commercial class which soon discovered the connection between strong government at home and commercial privileges abroad. In some ways More himself was an important representative of this class, and often its spokesman. It was tragic that in the half century when the Church faced the triple challenge of commercialism, nationalism, and Lutheranism it was hampered in its efforts to answer them by its own corruption. The papacy was not then the spiritual institution which commands the world's respect to-day, but a worldly thing, at times even pagan, and as involved as any temporal prince in the rivalries in Italy, and meshed in the deceitful alliances hatched in the chancellories of Europe. It was a papacy doubly captive—to its own vices as well as to the ambitions of the powers.

More had the insight to see through the superficialities. Discredited though the papacy might be, what did it represent to England and Europe? More tells us constantly in his writings, and above all at his trial. There he appealed from the statutes of the English Parliament to the General Council of Christendom. He argued that a divinely ordained allegiance was sealed when Pope Gregory sent Augustine to England to claim it for the Christian fold. The faith we then embraced had been sworn to by every monarch since, and confirmed in Magna Carta. The

oath to uphold the Christian Church and to guarantee its liberties was not something to be cast aside because a temporal
prince could not get his way over a divorce. There was the
matter of damnation! Was there no peril to the soul in foment-
ing schism? The collective decisions of the Christendom to
which, by virtue of the conversion of England, we belonged,
could not be ignored. We are part, More insisted always, of
this Christendom, and to sever ourselves from it is not to be
thought of as a device to defeat a vacillating Pope! How could we
lightly dismember that which God Himself sought to establish?

The Papal supremacy was, in More's eyes, the guarantee of
the spiritual unity of Christendom. It was useless to pretend
that the Bishop of Rome was just as other bishops; to assert this
was to discredit Christ's word to Peter. And if Christendom
really existed, then it must have a head for the same reason that
a country had a prince: the head was either Pope, or General
Council, or Pope appointed by General Council. If the unity
was broken by denying the papal supremacy, then, no matter
what justifications might be produced for it, the victory was
one for the forces of darkness. They needed little encourage-
ment. More asserted that the surrender to the 'great Turk' within a nation meant ultimate victory for the infidel who was fighting his way up from Constantinople into the heart of Europe
in More's own lifetime, and whose menace was so little understood that one Pope at least was prepared to make an alliance
with the Turks in order to defeat his European enemies, and
the Lutherans would rather the Turks had Rome than the
Popes. Such was the measure of European folly. The papal
supremacy and European unity went together, destroy the one
and it would be impossible ever again to guarantee the other;
disorder and dissension would increase everywhere, and Christ's
church itself be endangered. In disowning his debt to Europe,
Henry VIII was turning his back on European civilization, and
More was virtually the only layman in England who saw what
it all implied for the future.

## 'DISCORD AND DISSENSION'

Henry VIII would not have accepted this reading of his behaviour, of course, and few other Englishmen either. More was quite misunderstood at the time of his martyrdom. It seemed a little thing to many of his family and friends to swear the oath about the supremacy. Why should he not swear? He might have reservations, as many others had, but England was a Christian country, and would always be so; kings did not last for ever, and all things adjusted themselves in time. And indeed, the Statutes of Provisors and Praemunire of 1351 and 1352 had established already, in some sense, the 'supremacy' of the king over the Church in England. Many must have thought that the claim of Henry VIII to the obedience of the Church was, the royal divorce apart, a logical and inevitable development of earlier assertions of English independence of Rome. 'The crown of England, . . . has been so free at all times, that it has been in no earthly subjection, but immediately subject to God,' the Statute of Praemunire said, and the King's latest claim seemed no more a menace to the unity of Christendom than this earlier assertion had proved. It is More's genius that he saw what it all implied *in the long run* and went to his death rather than be a party to it.

It has been a pretty long run. The sixteenth century did not understand. Has any century understood what was then involved, until our own? For our century has seen the triumph of the secular, nationalist state, the rise of bloody and fanatical ideologies, the ruin of that Europe born in the sixteenth century. And now, at the possibility of its total loss, we see—at last, at last we see—how precious is that European civilization which is Christianity's gift, and how little likely it is to survive without the support of the threatened faith. Only now we learn the frightful alternatives. It is the irony of history that our century seeks to restore by secular alliances and unions the spiritual unity which the sixteenth so lightly cast away.

Henry's victory was not a paper one: its ruthless exploitation

21

by the efficient disciple of the new power politics, Thomas
Cromwell, involved tremendous social consequences. The link
with Rome was irreparably broken, the Church made humble
and subservient, the monastic orders ruined and dispersed and
their lands looted, spoiled, alienated. A priceless heritage of
beauty, above all of architectural beauty, was lost. The Christian order had vanished, and if now the poor wanted shelter, or
the sick support, they would look in vain for the institutions
which could provide it. They had become the property of the
new commercial classes, or of the King's men, or else roofless
ruins. In vain the young men looked for havens where a life of
worship, contemplation or study could be lived. The young
man without means has had to wait until this mid-century for
that social and cultural assistance any poor peasant's son with
brains could have had for the asking in the fifteenth century.
We can conceive no parallel in our own times to the Crom-
wellian plunder unless we can imagine, overnight, the welfare
state done away with, the public libraries abolished, the loot
distributed among commissars, and a new mad material
scramble forced upon us all in a land where it was best to hold
your tongue about everything important.⌉

   The historian Pollard wrote: 'The nation purchased political
salvation at the price of moral debasement; the individual was
sacrificed on the altar of the State; and popular subservience
proved the impossibility of saving a people from itself. Con-
stitutional guarantees are worthless without the national will
to maintain them; men lightly abandon what they lightly hold;
and, in Henry's reign, the English spirit of independence
burned low in its socket, and love of freedom grew cold.'[1]

   At the end of his reign Henry VIII read his faithful Parliament a reproachful sermon. He thanked them for the kindness
they had ever manifested towards him (as well he might), and
because of it he could not choose but love and favour them.
Nevertheless, all was not well. 'Charity and Concord is not
amongst you, but Discord and Dissensions beareth rule in

every place. .... Behold then, what love and charity is amongst
you, when one calleth another heretic and anabaptist, and he
calleth him again papist, hypocrite and Pharisee? Be these
tokens of Charity amongst you? Are these signs of fraternal love
amongst you? . . . I hear daily that you of the clergy preach one
against another, without charity or discretion; some be too stiff
in their old *Mumpsimus*, others be too busy and curious in their
new *Sumpsimus*. . . . I am very sorry to know and to hear how
unreverently that most precious jewel, the Word of God, is
disputed, rhymed, sung, and jangled in every Ale-house and
Tavern. . . . And yet I am even as much sorry that the readers
of the same follow it in doing, so faintly and so coldly. For of
this I am sure, that charity was never so faint amongst you,
and virtuous and godly living was never less used, nor God
Himself among Christians was never less reverenced, honoured
or served.'

Every revolution has its price.

# CHAPTER TWO

# FIRST PAGE, THEN SCHOLAR

Thomas More was born in Milk Street, in the city of London, on 6th February 1478, the second child of a prosperous, *bourgeois* city family, with some country property in Hertfordshire, awarded the right to armorial bearings at a date not known. His father, John More, was butler or steward to Lincoln's Inn, a post which had come down to him from Thomas's grandfather, another Thomas More: like him, John More was admitted to the society in recognition of his services, and in 1517, at the time of his son's rising fame, was awarded a judgeship. He died in 1530, before his son's fatal clash with Henry VIII.

However, there are some doubts about Thomas More's ancestry—city records reveal many of the name of More—and a writer in the *Times Literary Supplement*[1] recently sought to identify 'More's grandfather as a William More, but baker not scrivener, of London, not Bristol, and probably of a later generation than More the scrivener'.

Holbein's drawing of Sir John More, at Windsor Castle, shows a firm, resolute old man with a shrewd, humorous eye in his weather-beaten face—the face of a sailor or traveller rather than lawyer. Looking at his portrait we can understand the jest for which he, four times married, was famous, that matrimony was a perilous choice, all of a piece with putting 'your hand into a blind bag full of snakes and eels, seven snakes for one eel'.

We catch a glimpse of an obscure member of John More's

household in *Dialogue of Comfort against Tribulation*, written by
Thomas More in the Tower in the last year of his life. 'My
mother had (when I was a little boy) a good old woman that
took heed to her children, they called her mother Mawde. . . .
She was wont when she sat by the fire with us, to tell us (that
were children) many childish tales. But as Plinius saith that
there is no book lightly so bad, but that some good thing a man
may pike thereof, so think I that there is almost no tale so foolish, but that yet in one matter or other, to some purpose it may
hap to serve. For I remember that among other of her fond
tales, she told us once, that the Ass and the Wolf came upon a
time to confession to the Fox.' It's a tale almost out of Uncle
Remus, and if indeed it were told for children, it illustrates how
completely the lives of the youngest were absorbed in the
duties of the Church, and how free the talk about Christian
matters could be round a homely fireside.

The poor Ass hurries to confess to the Fox long before Ash
Wednesday, but the Wolf delays almost till Good Friday. The
Ass makes foolish haste because he is over-scrupulous, full of
self-torment about trivialities, and afraid he may miss the benefits of priestly intercessions unless he is early on the scene. And
his confessor 'was so weary to sit so long and hear him, that
saving for the manner sake, he had liever have sitten all that
while at breakfast with a good fat goose'. The Wolf, however,
delayed his confession until the last moment for fear that he
might be compelled to give penance for his gluttony and so be
deprived of pleasure for an inordinate length of time. The confessor admits, man to man, that he does not bother about fasts
himself—they are not from God, but are inventions of man—
and the talk between the pair turns on the price of poultry. The
penance which is set upon the worldly Wolf is that he shall
never pay more than sixpence for a meal, whereas it is *upon the
Ass* that the penance for gluttony is laid. This is a subtle tale
indeed to have impressed itself upon the young Thomas, and
we meet a variation of it again in Thomas More's life, at the

time of his imprisonment, when, on the lips of his successor to the Chancellorship, it is used as a warning to More not to judge the King by himself—leave to the Wolf what belongs to the Wolf's nature, and do not interfere, but beware, O Ass, of imagining, because all is conceded to the Wolf, even one step out of line is permitted to you!

Maybe it was from mother Maud that More garnered the other stories which adorn so much of the *Dialogue*, the fables from Aesop, and such terrifying tales, with a medieval maliciousness about them, as that of the shrewish wife who goaded and tormented her carpenter husband, even to the point of laying her head upon his block when he had an axe in his hand, and defying him to behead her—which he did, for he could not bear to be unmanned any longer. Or perhaps this came from the gossip of his lawyer father about strange cases?

Though Thomas's first learning was in folk wisdom, he was presently taught his Latin at St. Anthony's Hospital in Threadneedle Street, a famous school under a famous master, Nicholas Holt—

> *A little schoole of Christen folk there stood*
> *Down at the further end, in which there were*
> *Children an heep comen of Cristen blood,*
> *That learned in that schoole, year by year,*
> *Such manner doctrine as men used there;*
> *That is to say, to sing and eke to read,*
> *As smalle children do in their childhede.*

and we can picture him, like Chaucer's 'little clergeon, seven years of age', 'his little book learning, As he sat in the school at his primer', yet not so dutiful and meek that he could not regret the hours lost to play. When, as a youth, Thomas 'devised in his father's house in London, a goodly hanging of fine-painted cloth, with nine pageants, and verses over every of those pageants', he devoted the first to Childhood. The tapestry showed a boy whipping his top, and Master Thomas's lines above it read:

# FIRST PAGE, THEN SCHOLAR

*I am called Childhood, in play is all my mind,*
*To cast a coit, a cokstele, and a ball.*
*A top can I set, and drive it in his kind,*
*But would to God these hatefull bookes all,*
*Were in a fire burnt to powder small.*
*Then might I lead my life always in play:*
*Which life god send me to mine ending day.*[a]

There is nothing perfunctory about those lines: they are the
heart-sent and fervent cry of boyhood. And though in the
tapestry of Manhood, which comes next, the boy is ridden
down by 'a goodly fresh young man, riding upon a goodly
horse, having an hawk on his fist' Childhood still squats between the horse's feet, clinging to his top and his whip, for
'thinketh this boy his peevish game sweeter' than all the hunt-
ing in the world. 'But what no force, his reason is no better.'

Stow records, in his *Survey of London*, that the St. Anthony's
of his day held yearly disputations with the scholars of other
schools on St. Bartholomew's eve in the churchyard of St.
Bartholomew, Smithfield, and that the scholars of St. Anthony's usually won the prizes. The rivalry between St. Anthony's and the St. Paul's school founded (long after More's
childhood) by Colet caused the scholars of the two schools as
often as they met to throw down their satchels and come to
blows, scuffling up and down the lanes to the discomfort of the
citizenry and the obstruction of the traffic in the narrow streets.
Then, as now, the pigeons flocked around St. Paul's (the old
St. Paul's) and 'Paul's pigeons' warred against the 'Anthony
Pigs'. No doubt the Anthony pigs found others to annoy in
Thomas's childhood.

The hours given to lessons in sixteenth-century schools were
long. Boarders were early to rise and early to bed, and day boys
had to conform to their discipline. If Winchester School is any
guide, the rising bell was rung at five in the morning. The
scholars had to gather to sing a Latin hymn when it ceased, and

so had to hurry into their clothes. There followed many ses-
sions of school before, at 8.15, they were finally in bed again.
If the curriculum of St. Anthony's was like this, then the following dialogue from one of the Colloquies of Erasmus might
be applied to Thomas's schooldays:

'Sylvius: Why are you in such a hurry, John?

'Joannes: Why does the hare run before the hounds, as they say?

'Sylvius: What does that proverb mean?

'Joannes: That if I'm not in time for roll-call, it is all up with
my skin.

'Sylvius: You needn't be afraid, it has just gone five. Look
at the hands of the clock.

'Joannes: H'm, I don't much trust clocks. They tell lies
sometimes.

'Sylvius: But you can trust me who heard it strike five.

'Joannes: But being late's not the only thing to be afraid of;
I have to say off by heart yesterday's lesson, a pretty stiff one;
and I am not sure if I know it.

'Sylvius: We are in the same boat, for I'm not very well up
in mine.

'Joannes: And you know what a beast our master is, down
on us at every chance to tan our hides as if they were a bull's.

'Sylvius: But he won't be at school to-day. Cornelius is
coming instead of him.

'Joannes: That cross-eyed fellow! Then our backs will smart
for it; he's worse than Orbilius at licking.

'Sylvius: That's a fact; and I've often prayed that his arm
might be paralysed.'[3]

And indeed there is a passage in More's *Dialogue of Comfort*
where, to illustrate the moral cowardice which avoids plain-
speaking to princes about the rocks ahead, he uses, out of painful memories of the past, the story of the mother 'which when
the little boy will not rise in time for her, but lie still a bed and
slugg, and when he is up, weepeth because he hath lien so long,
fearing to be beaten at school for his late coming thither: she

telleth him that then it is but early days, and he shall come time enough and biddeth him "Go, good son, I warrant thee, I have sent to thy master myself, take thy bread and butter with thee, thou shalt not be beaten at all". And thus, so she may send him merry forth at the door that he weep not in her sight at home, she studieth not much upon the matter, though he be taken tardy and beaten when he cometh to school.'[4]

We need not doubt that little Thomas, though he learnt his Latin, had his fill 'of evil schoolmasters, which be readier to beat, than to teach scholars'. And as to the schoolmasters themselves, Erasmus satirises them wickedly in *In Praise of Folly* in a passage which says little for the scholars either: they are, he alleges, 'always damned to thurst and hunger, to be choaked with dust in their unswept schools (schools shall I term them, or rather elaboratories, nay, bridewells, and houses of correction?) to wear themselves in fret and drudgery; to be deafened with the noise of gaping boys, and in short, to be stifled with heat and stench, and yet they cheerfully dispense with all these inconveniences, and, by the help of a fond conceit, think themselves as happy as any thing living; taking a great pride and delight in frowning and looking big upon the trembling urchins, in boxing, slashing, striking with the ferula, and in the exercise of all their other methods of tyranny; while thus lording it over a parcel of young, weak chits, they imitate the Cuman ass, and think themselves as stately as a lion, that domineers over all the inferior herd.' They can submit to any degree of filth and nastiness, and to the most intolerable smells, so long as their vanity is puffed up by their role of authority. And if one of them lights upon some old unusual word, or some curious but little known fact, 'or can, after a great deal of poring, spell out the inscription of some battered monument, Lord! what joy, what triumph, what congratulating their success, as if they had conquered Africa, or taken Babylon the Great!'[5]

Thomas Elyot, who wrote the first book in English on education, complained in More's day of the damage done by ignorant schoolmasters, and John Colet in the Statutes he drew up for St. Paul's school inveighed against the barbarous and adulterate Latin then taught; and all such abused Latin 'which more rather may be called "blotterature" than literature' he utterly banished from his school. If the learning was corrupt and the discipline sadistic, what did the young get from their schooldays? It is sometimes difficult to imagine when Erasmus relates that often after a common meal a schoolmaster would pick out a boy and hand him over for punishment to a bircher, who would not let the boy go till he fell half insensible at his feet. The teacher would then turn calmly to the scholars and say, 'True, he has done nothing, but he must be humiliated'.

If, later in the same century, Roger Ascham, who was tutor to Princess, later Queen Elizabeth, was to be found arguing in *The Scholemaster* that gentle correction and the spirit of love were better fitted than violence to encourage the young in learning, that was in no small measure due to the attitude of More, Colet, Erasmus and their humanist circle. They were great educational reformers.

It was the practice of medieval chivalry to send a boy as a page to the household of another, there to wait at table and at bedside, to be apprenticed in good manners and courtly ways, and, if fortunate, to learn some letters. When very young, the child, prettily dressed, would wait upon the ladies, and be petted by them, but as he grew he would become valet to the lord, serve in the stables, learn the exercises of war and of the chase, and become in the end the squire whom we meet everywhere in medieval romances who sighed for his lady while he proved himself for the degree of knighthood. This practice had not died out by the end of the fifteenth century, though the rise of regular schools, where boys might board, and the degeneration of chivalry itself had brought about a considerable decline in the custom.

# FIRST PAGE, THEN SCHOLAR

Young Thomas More, at the age of twelve, was fortunate
enough to be received, by his father's influence, according to
Roper's *Life*, 'into the house of the right reverend, wise and
learned prelate Cardinal Morton'—at that time not yet cardinal
but Lord Chancellor of England. It was as if a bright lawyer's
son to-day were to be brought up at the White House, or 10
Downing Street. Thomas made an impression on the household, for there 'though he was young of years, would he at
Christmastide suddenly sometimes step in among the players,
and never studying for the matter, made a part of his own there
presently among them, which made the lookers-on more sport
than all the players beside. In whose wit and towardness the
Cardinal much delighting, would often say of him unto the
nobles that divers times dined with him, "This child here waiting at table, whosoever shall live to see it, will prove a marvellous man".'

In the pages of *Utopia* More has left us a picture of his bene-
factor as a man 'not more honourable for his authority, than
for his prudence and virtue. He was of a mean stature, and
though stricken in age, yet bare he his body upright. In his face
did shine such an amiable reverence, as was pleasant to behold,
gentle in communication, yet earnest and sage. He had great
delight many times with rough speech to his suitors, to prove,
but without harm, what prompt wit and what bold spirit were
in every man. In the which, as in a virtue much agreeing with
his nature, so that therewith were not joined impudence, he
took great delectation. And the same person, as apt and meet
to have an administration in the weal public, he did lovingly
embrace. In his speech he was fine, eloquent, and pithy. In the
law he had profound knowledge, in wit he was incomparable,
and in memory wonderful excellent. These qualities, which in
him were by nature singular, he by learning and use had made
perfect. The king put much trust in his counsel, the weal public
also in a manner leaned unto him, when I was there.' The
Cardinal is spoken of in More's *Richard the Third* as 'of

great natural wit, very well learned, and honourable in behaviour'. And his influence upon the boy is demonstrated by the fact that, in *Utopia*, More sets his remarkable discussion of the social conditions in England at the Cardinal's table.

Though the burden of the discourse in *Utopia* is placed in the mouth of Ralph Hythloday, the narrator of the travels to Utopia, and More puts himself in, in the first person, mostly as an interlocutor, all the thought is Thomas More's, of course. And when he makes Hythloday say that he 'durst boldly speak' his mind before the Cardinal, it is authentic autobiography we are listening to. Thus the boy had been commanded to speak up by the master who recognized his genius. And though More skilfully contrived his arguments to give them an air of verisimilitude, yet among the discussions are some which read like reports of things long remembered. Such surely is the derision poured by the jester upon idle friars, and the indignant reply of 'a certain friar, graduate in divinity' which provoked a rebuke from the Cardinal. We are told that when an angry and boorish argument looked like having no end, the Cardinal sent away 'the jester by a privy beck' and turned the conversation to another matter. We are here watching the behaviour of men at the tables of the greatest in the land through the eyes of an impressionable boy already making his judgments of men, seeing through their follies and cheats, and forming for himself, with Morton as his exemplar, his own remarkable standards of rectitude and courtesy.

Archbishop Morton, in his seventieth year in 1490, must have seemed a legendary figure to a boy avid to learn his country's history, for the old man was in some degree the architect of the Tudor rule. A Lancastrian supporter, he had lived with the exiled court of Margaret of Anjou and taken part in the battle of Tewkesbury which destroyed the Lancastrian hopes. After that he made his peace with Edward IV. He was entrusted with several royal diplomatic missions, and in 1479 elected to the bishopric of Ely. As an executor of

Edward IV's will he was hated by Richard Crookback, arrested by him, but skilfully extricating himself from the usurper's hands made his way to France to support the cause of young Richmond. And when the Earl of Richmond triumphed on Bosworth field, and was crowned Henry VII, Morton emerged as his principal counsellor. Honours fell thick upon him—he was made Archbishop of Canterbury in 1473, Lord Chancellor three years before Thomas More entered his household, and Cardinal in 1493 when Thomas had left him.

Morton's influence shines through More's *Richard the Third* (sometimes entitled *The Pitiful Life of King Edward the Fifth* since it stops short, unfinished, soon after the murder of the princes in the Tower), and even if we need not suppose that the work is a translation of a Latin Chronicle by Morton, we have to acknowledge that it must have been from Morton that More derived most of his knowledge. Certainly the lessons of Morton's career bit deep into young More's soul, for from the earliest days his writings are full of an acute sense of the hazards of high office and of the treacherous love of princes.

Roper tells us that Morton placed the young scholar (and disciple, too, surely?) at Oxford, at Canterbury Hall, afterwards absorbed into Wolsey's foundation, Christ Church. Thomas was then about fourteen, and proficient in Latin, and he may have begun to learn Greek under Grocyn, who had brought Greek letters to England and was the first to teach them publicly, and from Thomas Linacre, too, who was to become his close friend. It is certain that More regarded his two years at Oxford as the hardest time of his life. In all probability the Archbishop's board had ill-prepared him for the poverty and hardship of student life. The discipline of the universities towards the end of the fifteenth century was as severe as that of the schools. The undergraduates were supervised as closely as schoolboys. The student was compelled to hear mass and say mattins and vespers every day. If he did not he was fined. Manners and morals were likewise subject to a tariff, it cost fourpence in fines to indulge in sword-play, and a farthing to swear: this was the rate of payment, too, for speaking English, bringing an unsheathed knife to table, or going into the fields unaccompanied by a fellow-student! Sleeping out without leave was taxed fourpence. The tariff is endless, and to understand the severity of the fines we must multiply them by nearly twenty.

We do not know whether the Archbishop made Thomas an allowance; there was no reason to, for Thomas's father was not a poor man. But John More, all the same, seems deliberately to have kept his son on a tight string, so that he would have had no money for dissipation, even had the close university discipline permitted it. So close that he could not even pay for the mending of his shoes, and had to send home for the money! And this probably meant, on the Oxford commons of those days, that he went continually hungry. More by no means resented his father's parsimony, and in after life would say, 'It was thus that I indulged in no vice or pleasure, and spent my time in no vain or hurtful amusements; I did not know what luxury meant, and never learnt to use money badly; in a word, I loved and thought of nothing but my studies.'

In fact, More, abstemious by nature, was inclined to frugality. Erasmus wrote of him that he was, 'as a young man . . . by preference a water drinker, a practice he derived from his father. But not to give annoyance to others, he used at table to conceal this habit from his guests by drinking out of a pewter vessel, either small beer almost as weak as water, or plain water. As to wine, it being the custom where he was for the company to invite each other to drink in turn of the same cup, he used sometimes to sip a little of it, to avoid appearing to shrink from it altogether, and to habituate himself to the common practice. For his eating he has been accustomed to prefer beef and salt meats, and household bread thoroughly fermented to those articles of diet which are commonly regarded as delicacies.'

The paternal severity, if such it was, made no breach in his

relations with his father. One biographer, Stapleton, relates
how More maintained his filial reverence when he was made
Chancellor and did not hesitate publicly, in the palace of Westminster, to kneel down and ask his father's blessing, 'according
to the excellent custom of our country'. Yet the observance of
'excellent customs', gracious though they may be, would tell
us little of the real relations between father and son, were they
all. But we need not doubt that in More's intimate and tender
relations with his own children is to be found the mirror of
the fond friendship with his father. The boy whose wit and intelligence impressed the Archbishop's table must have been
excellent company, and with his shrewd and humorous father
must often have been very merry. Young Thomas certainly
did not lack impudence. Richard Pace, secretary to Henry
VIII, recorded that his friend More once heard two famous
Scotist theologians seriously discussing the legend that King
Arthur made a cloak of the beards of the giants he had killed
in battle. 'When More asked them how that could be, the elder
of the two, putting on a grave countenance, replied: "The
reason, my youth, is clear, for the skin of a dead man is elastic."
The other, hearing this, not only assented, but admired the answer as subtle and Scotistic. More was but a boy, but he answered: "What you say was hitherto quite as unknown to me
as it was perfectly well known that one of you milks a he-goat
while the other holds a sieve." When he saw that they did not
understand his meaning, he laughed to himself, and went his
way.' However, Pace seems to have been the earnest kind of
young man who could not see that young Thomas was having
his leg pulled, too, and far more subtly.[6]

Thomas did not stay long enough at the university to take
his degree. In 1494 he was brought back to London to be entered at New Inn. Why? It was not unusual in those days to
leave the university before taking a degree, but Thomas was,
after all, the Archbishop's nominee, and ecclesiastical prefer-
ment could have been his had he taken holy orders, and it must

have been with this intention that he was sent to Canterbury Hall. The recall to London may have been due to some tug-of-war over the boy's career. This is not wholly guess-work, for Erasmus suggests that the cause of his precipitate removal from Oxford was because he entered too deeply into the new learning, to the neglect of the law studies for which his father designed him; he wrote that More 'had drunk deep of Good Letters from his earliest years; and when a young man he applied himself to the study of Greek and Philosophy; but his father was so far from encouraging him in this pursuit, that he withdrew his allowance and almost disowned him, because he thought he was deserting his hereditary study, being himself an expert professor of English law.' Nevertheless, it does not seem that More suffered in any way, certainly not in diet, by his transfer 'to an Inn of Chancery, called New Inn, where for his time, he very well prospered'. Roper goes on to tell us that from thence he 'was committed to Lincoln's Inn, with very small allowance, continuing there his study until he was made and accounted a worthy utter barrister'. The second transfer took place in 1496, when he was eighteen.

More prospered so well in his studies that upon his becoming a barrister he was appointed reader or lecturer in the science of law to Furnivall's Inn. He did not neglect his literary and theological pursuits in the new learning, and it is most remarkable to find that in his very early twenties he delivered a series of lectures on St. Augustine's *City of God* in Dr. Grocyn's church of St. Lawrence, Old Jewry. It must have been at Dr. Grocyn's proposal that these lectures were delivered, and they were attended by him, and were well remembered and regarded. One can think of no better preparation for the writing of *Utopia* than such a study and it is a loss to literature that none of the series has survived. By this time More and Erasmus had become friends, for Erasmus paid his first visit to England in 1499, and in that year was already corresponding with More and speaking of him as his dear friend. It is a remarkable tribute to the great esteem in which More was held, even as a boy of twenty-one, that in 1499, as we shall presently relate, he was in a position to present Erasmus to the royal children at Eltham Palace.

In his eighteenth year, Roper records, Thomas More 'gave himself to devotion and prayer in the Charterhouse of London, religiously living there without vow for about four years' as though the struggle about a career which might have caused his premature withdrawal from Oxford had finally come to a crisis, and he was considering taking monastic vows. It is in this sense that Cresacre More, his great-grandson, expands the cursory sentence with which Roper disposes of the spiritual crisis of More's youth. 'When he was about eighteen or twenty years old, finding his body, by reason of his years, most rebellious, he sought diligently to tame his unbridled concupiscence by wonderful works of mortification. He used often time to wear a sharp shirt of hair next to his skin, which he never left off wholly—no, not when he was Lord Chancellor of England' (it was this shirt, or a successor, which he sent home to his daughter Margaret from the Tower, on the day before his martyrdom, and which is treasured as a relic by the Augustinian Canonesses of Abbot's Leigh, in Devonshire). 'He used also much fasting and watching, lying often either upon the bare ground or upon some bench, or laying some log under his head, allotting himself but four or five hours in a night at the most for his sleep, imagining with the holy saints of Christ's Church, that his body was to be used like an ass, with strokes and hard fare, lest provender might prick it, and so bring his soul like a headlong jade into the bottomless pit of hell. For chastity, especially in youth, is a lingering martyrdom, and these are the best means to preserve her from the dangerous gulf of evil custom. But he is the best soldier in this fight that can run fastest away from himself, this victory being hardly gotten with striving. He had inured himself to the straitness that he might the better enter the narrow gates of heaven, which is not got with ease, *sed violenti rapiunt illud*, that is to say, they that are boisterous against themselves, bear it away by force. For this cause he lived for four years amongst the Carthusians, dwelling near the Charterhouse, frequenting daily their spiritual exercises, but without any vow. He had an earnest mind also to be a Franciscan friar, that he might serve God in a state of perfection; but, finding that at that time religious men in England had somewhat degenerated from their ancient strictness, and fervour of spirit, he altered his mind.'[7]

Was it for his own fault, or the fault of others, that he changed his mind? Again, Erasmus is our guide. He says that More 'applied his whole mind to exercise of piety, looking to and pondering on the priesthood in vigils, fasts, and prayers, and similar austerities. In which matter he proved himself far more prudent than most candidates, who thrust themselves rashly into the arduous profession, without any previous trial of their powers. The one thing that prevented him from giving himself to that kind of life was that he could not shake off the desire of the married state. He chose, therefore, to be a chaste husband rather than an impure priest.'

And this seems nearer the truth. It is wise to read into More's rejection of monastic vows or of the priesthood a criticism of neither, but rather a sense of his own unworthiness. His tender regard, and praise for, the Carthusians of London continued all his life, and he shared their martyrdom, and wrote, to the very end, of the life of withdrawal from the world as something for which he had never lost his longing. And Cresacre More, in that passage I have quoted, goes on to speak of More as having another vocation to fulfil. 'He had also after that together with his faithful companion Lilly a purpose to be a priest; yet God had allotted him for another estate, not to live solitary, but that he might be a pattern to married men how they should carefully bring up their children, how dearly they should love their wives, how they should employ their endeavour wholly for the good of their country, yet excellently perform the virtues of religious men, as piety, charity, humility, obedience and conjugal chastity.'

To this vocation he remained faithful, and his house at Chelsea became a platonic academy, an Utopia in little, of sons and daughters, sons-in-law, grandchildren, secretaries, retainers, students, jester and zoo, and the painter Holbein was to immortalize it.

When More was thirty-six he met again one who, as a girl, had captured his heart. He had suffered his boyish pangs for her at the age of sixteen, when he was a poor student at New Inn, and upon meeting his old love again celebrated it in a nostalgic poem 'To Eliza, whom he had loved in his Youth'. More's marriages were not love affairs; nevertheless, he was so susceptible to the demands of the flesh that he regarded them as, in him, a barrier to the monastic or priestly life. His tender remembrance of times past is his only recorded love affair. In it he rejoices that

> *Thou liv'st, Eliza, to these eyes restored,*
> *O more than life, if life's gay bloom, adored.*
> *Many a long year, since first we met, has rolled,*
> *I then was boyish, and now am old.*
> *Scarce had I bid my sixteenth summer hail,*
> *And two in thine were wanting to the tale,*
> *When thy soft mien—ah, mien for ever fled!—*
> *On my tranced heart its guiltless influence shed.*
>
> *Now on my memory breaks that happy day,*
> *When first I saw thee with thy mates at play;*
> *On thy white neck the flaxen ringlet lies,*
> *With snow thy cheek, thy lip with roses vies.*
> *Thine eyes, twin stars, with arrowy radiance shine,*
> *And pierce and sink into my heart through mine.*
> *Struck as with heaven's own bolt, I stand, I gaze,*
> *I hang upon thy look in fixed amaze.*

# FIRST PAGE, THEN SCHOLAR

*And as I writhe beneath the new-felt spear,*
*My artless pangs our young companions jeer.*

The secret was not kept—

*For one who knew with what chaste warmth you burned*
*Had blabbed the secret of my love returned.*
*—Then the duenna and the guarded door*
*Baffled the stars, and bade us meet not more.*

*Crimeless, my heart you stole in love's soft prime,*
*And still possess that heart without a crime.*
*Pure was the love which in my youth prevailed,*
*And age would keep it pure, if honour failed.*[8]

The poem ends with an invocation to the gods that they may meet again and hail each other when another 'five long lustres' have passed. In just that time More was dead. There is no evidence for it, but there may be those who will wish to connect More's struggle to take monastic vows with the loss of Eliza to 'the duenna and the guarded door'.

Thomas More was already writing as a youth and may first have achieved print at the age of nineteen. We cannot say when he wrote the little homilies in verse for the tapestries hung in his father's house, but other compositions can be traced at least as far back as the year 1503, when he was twenty-five. One of them, it is alleged, is *These Fowre Things*, a jest about how a sergeant-at-law dressed himself up as a friar in order to make an arrest for debt. It is clearly written to be recited, perhaps as a prologue to the Sergeants' Feast of 1503 when John More was elected Sergeant-at-Law, perhaps as a prologue to a series of plays or masques. To associate it with John More's election would be a reasonable enough notion, except that it is all cast in a mood far too juvenile to associate with the scholar and barrister who had already delivered learned lectures on Augustine's *The City of God*, and who was on the eve of election to

40

Parliament. For lack of evidence one cannot place it as far back as the days in Archbishop Morton's palace when young Thomas loved to step among the players and improvize a part, but it must derive from his experiences of those days, and it is certainly close in spirit and technical accomplishment to the rhymes written for the tapestries in his father's house, and like them must be the product of his adolescence. In William Rastell's famous black-letter edition of *The Works of Sir Thomas More* (1557) the jest is simply attributed to More's youth, and no date is given to it. Erasmus tells us that the youthful More wrote and acted in his own plays: this must be a sample of them. And though this does not prevent us from imagining that the jest was performed at a Sergeants' feast, the long legal associations of the More family would have made it a suitable skit for a gathering of his father's friends at almost any time.

The story of *These Fowre Things* is that a young man wastes his inheritance, gets into debt and then hides himself in the house of a friend under the pretext of being

> *So sick alway,*
> *He might not come abroad.*

The problem was, and it throws light upon English common law in the sixteenth century, how to get to him and serve a warrant for his arrest. A brave sergeant undertakes the task and disguises himself as a friar and so dressed betakes himself to the debtor's house, and persuades the maid to ask the man if he will receive 'an austen fryre' who 'would with hym speke'. He is brought up to the sick room, and there in the presence of the maid hypocritically takes the man's hands and begins to speak words of comfort, but the moment the girl departs says 'I arrest thee' and takes out his mace.

The sick man replies by hitting him in the ear, and in a moment the pair are brawling on the floor. The maid and the housewife rush upstairs to break up the fight, and they pull the

friar's hood over the sergeant's face, give him a great beating
and

> *Up hym they lift*
> *And with yll thrift,*
> *Hedlyng a long the stayre*
> *Down him they threwe . . .*

And the moral of this knock-about comedy is that the cob-
bler should stick to his last:

> *When an hatter*
> *Will go smatter,*
> *In philosophy,*
> *Or a pedlar*
> *Waxe a medlar,*
> *In theology*

the consequence is sure to be that he 'will beshrewe himselfe at
last'.

In 1503 Henry VII's wife, Queen Elizabeth, the mother of
Henry VIII, died, and Thomas More composed a lament which
begins:

> *O ye that put your trust and confidence,*
> *In worldly joy and frail prosperity,*
> *That so live here as ye should never hence,*
> *Remember death and look here upon me.*
> *Ensample I think there may no better be.*
> *Your self wot well that in this realm was I*
> *Your queen but late, and lo now here I lie.*

The poem continues, a conventional lamentation and farewell in the first person. It is not great poetry, but yet evidence
of Thomas More's truly Shakespearian consciousness of the
pathos of the collapse of greatness through sickness or death, or
the tragedy of its undoing through fortune or ambition. It was
an awareness which was to grow with the years, yet it is to be
found quite explicitly stated as a theme in verses he wrote for

a popular publishing venture, *The Book of Fortune*, about the same time. More does not despise in these verses the opportunities which fortune brings to a man, and makes Fortune herself say:

> *But he that by my favour may ascend,*
> *To mighty power and excellent degree,*
> *A common weal to govern and defend,*
> *O in how blest condition standeth he:*
> *Himself in honour and felicity,*
> *And over that, may further and increase,*
> *A region whole in joyful rest and peace.*

But he adds his own warning, from 'Thomas More to them that trust in fortune' which in a vivid image speaks of those who would force the goddess to yield to them:

> *But lord how he doth think himself full wele.*
> *That may set once his hand upon her wheel.*
> *He holdeth fast: but upward as he flieth,*
> *She whippeth her wheel about, and there he lieth.*
>
> *Thus fell Julius from his mighty power.*
> *Thus fell Darius the worthy king of Perse.*
> *Thus fell Alexander the great conqueror.*
> *Thus many more than I may well rehearse.*
> *Thus double fortune, when she list reverse*
> *Her slipper favour them that in her trust,*
> *She fleeth away and layeth them in the dust.*
>
> *She suddenly enhanceth them aloft.*
> *And suddenly mischieveth all the flock.*
> *The head that late lay easily and full soft,*
> *In stead of pillows lieth after on the block.*

The man who trusts in fortune is a slave and only he is free who chooses to renounce fortune and live in humble poverty.

Such was the life of the philosophers and sages, Socrates, Aristippus, Pythagoras and even poor Diogenes in his tub, trying to keep in the sun:

> *Wherefore if thou in surety list to stand,*
> *Take poverty's part and let proud fortune go,*
> *Receive nothing that cometh from her hand:*
> *Love manner and virtue: they be only tho*
> *Which double fortune may not take thee fro.*

It would be unwise to read a prophetic sense into these lines; it is not the prophecy but the *wisdom* of the young man which is so uncanny. The young, even when entering upon a dangerous career, feel magnificently clothed against disaster by their own virility, and they dismiss it as an evil which cannot happen to them, or weigh the risks against the possibilities of great rewards, and feel they are worth taking. But from the beginning More held worldly rewards as of little worth, his mind was continually set upon other ones. No man, therefore, can have entered public life with fewer illusions or clearer knowledge of its perils.

CHAPTER THREE

# 'A PARLOUS WISE FELLOW'

Already, in his extreme youth, Thomas More belonged to the group of distinguished scholars and divines who have gone down to history as the Oxford Reformers. He was therefore not so much a product of the English Renaissance, as one of its creators, perhaps even its greatest leader. Whether the Renaissance proper can be said to date from the introduction of printing in 1440, or from the downfall of Constantinople in 1453, which scattered Byzantine scholars and classical manuscripts across Europe, is a matter we can leave to pedants to dispute. History itself provides evidence enough of the extraordinary transformation of Italian life and culture in the fifteenth century under the impact of the movement of liberation which carries the title of Renaissance, or re-birth. A re-birth it was, of classical learning to begin with, and then of the humanism and philosophies of ancient Greece and Rome, often seized upon without discrimination. It led to a new realistic and exuberant movement in art, to the birth of the sciences, to the rise in importance of the secular order, to the emergence of the sacred individual. Leonardo da Vinci, Michelangelo, Raphael, Erasmus, were its products. It produced a new conception of man, of man at home on earth as well as in heaven, man upstanding and self-governing, capable of mastering his earthly destiny and of creating a state, or social order, with the genius which belonged to a work of art.

This new view of man blossomed eventually into a notion that man was, so to speak, *natural* man, endowed with a moral-

ity which could be explained in terms of *natural* law rather than
revealed doctrine. It was expressed in the view that 'the man
who walked uprightly, and acted accordingly to the natural
law born within him, would go to heaven, whatever nation he
belonged to.'[1] In the same way was reborn the doctrine that
morality could be determined by the pleasure-pain principle;
what brought man pain, was bad; what brought him pleasure,
was good. We find this theory discussed in More's *Utopia*, for
instance; and that work is saturated also with the essentially
Renaissance concept of a rational and enterprising man, capable of determining his own destiny by reason of his inborn, or
natural gifts.

In Pico della Mirandola's 'Oration on the Dignity of Man'
the paganization so typical of the Renaissance had not gone so
deep. What we discover in that wonderful work is an exhilarating expansion of the Christian doctrine of man. And since
Pico was one of More's youthful heroes—he wrote an eulogis-
tic life of him—and his influence upon More's thought up to
the time of *Utopia* was very considerable, it is well worth
quoting a typical passage from the *Oration*:

'Then the Supreme Maker decreed,' Pico wrote, 'that unto
Man, on whom He could bestow nought singular, should belong in common whatsoever had been given to His other
creatures. Therefore He took man, made in His own individual
image, and having placed him in the centre of the world, spake
unto him thus: "Neither a fixed abode, nor a form in thine own
likeness, nor any gift peculiar to thyself alone, have we given
thee, O Adam, in order that what abode, what likeness, what
gifts thou shalt choose, may be thine to have and to possess.
The nature allotted to all other creatures, within laws appointed
by ourselves, restrains them. Thou, restrained by no narrow
bounds, according to thine own free will, in whose power I
have placed thee, shalt define thy nature for thyself. I have set
thee midmost the world, that thence thou mightest the more
conveniently survey whatsoever is in the world. Nor have we

made thee either heavenly or earthly, mortal or immortal, to the end that thou, being, as it were, thy own free maker and moulder, shouldst fashion thyself in what form may like thee best. Thou shalt have power to decline unto the lower or brute creatures. Thou shalt have power to be reborn unto the higher, or divine, according to the sentence of thy intellect." Thus to Man, at his birth, the Father gave seeds of all variety and germs of every form of life.'[2]

But the Renaissance which manifested such glorious confidence, perished in the most sickening corruption. Classical ideas, grotesquely exaggerated, became fads and fashions. Even the Church had to be 'classicized'; the Pope became *Pontifex Maximus*, the saints *Divus*, and almost translated to Olympus, and the Christian God became another Jupiter or Zeus. The paganization of the lived life of the Church went deeper, and Rome under that representative Borgia, Alexander VI, who died drinking from a poisoned cup he had prepared for someone else, was a labyrinth of vice and evil which can only be described as the antithesis of the Christianity of the saints and the apostles; and morally as remote as the Rome of Tiberius from the daily round of the simple, pious parish priest. Alexander VI secularized, and Leo X, the representative of the Medicis, who organized the sale of indulgences, commercialized the Church. It had become a cow to be milked. The inevitable consequence was the Reformation, the judgment of God upon a Church which had forgotten its holy mission. And for the Rome of learning and of curious sins, the end came in the sack of Rome in 1527 by Lutherans and equally savage Spaniards, who crucified poets upon trees and used the precious manuscripts of European learning to light their cooking fires.

Luther recoiled in horror from the glitter and wickedness of the Rome he visited. But such a shock cannot be discovered among the leaders of the English revival. For them the Roman pilgrimage was a revelation; they returned from it aroused and refreshed, enlightened by the new learning, and understanding

47

its role in the task of purifying the Church and its teachings, and revitalizing cultural and social life. The Italian Renaissance which moved them cannot have been quite so evil, at least in the manifestations which they encountered, as the Rome of the Borgias makes it appear. It did not undermine their faith, or disturb their intellect, or saddle them with the vices of the *Satyricon*. On the contrary, it purified and uplifted them, and made Christianity, by revealing more of its sources, new and wonderfully moving to them.

The connection of the English leaders with the Italian Renaissance was close. William Grocyn, Fellow of New College, Oxford, and a reader in Divinity at Magdalen, born *circa* 1446, visited Italy about 1488, and studied Greek and Latin at the feet of Demetrius Chalchondyles, the exiled Platonist from Athens, whose brother Laonicus was the historian of the Byzantine Empire. Demetrius began to teach first in Padua, then in the Florence of Lorenzo de Medici, barely ten years after the fall of Constantinople. He was associated with such scholars as Politian and Ficinus in the revival of Greek letters in Italy. One of his pupils was John Reuchlin, the scholar who carried Greek learning across the Alps to Heidelberg a few years after Grocyn brought it to Oxford. Linacre too, physician and divine, friend of Politian, went to school at Florence with the sons of Lorenzo de Medici, one of whom became Pope Leo X.

Grocyn's Oxford lectures on Greek learning began the movement others were to carry triumphantly forward. John Colet also made the journey to Italy and came back to deliver those Oxford lectures on the Pauline epistles which broke so effectively with the past by rejecting the allegorical treatment the Scriptures had received at the hands of medieval learning. Colet electrified the university by treating the Epistles as if they meant exactly what they said, and as if the most important problem was to come to that direct and unambiguous meaning. The life and teachings of Christ were for him the plain Christian faith and 'about the rest let divines dispute as they will'.

Colet's warm, almost homely Christianity so influenced Erasmus that we may say that it was Colet alone who prevented Erasmus from lapsing into the paganism so congenial to one side of his nature.

Colet is typical of the leaders of the English Renaissance in that he was quite unaffected by the paganism of the Italian movement, despite his sojourn in the Florence of Lorenzo the Magnificent. The new learning meant for Colet and More a purified and revived Christianity, strengthened by the discovery of the writings of the fathers, and illuminated by the philosophy of the Greeks. Colet's temper became almost puritan indeed; like More he caught something of the spirit of Savonarola. It was Colet who accompanied Erasmus on that historic religious pilgrimage to the tomb of St. Thomas of Canterbury, and denounced in no uncertain terms the display of wealth he found there. Colet, too, who denounced war from the pulpit of St. Paul's, proclaiming that 'an unjust peace is better than the justest war' and that 'when men out of hatred and ambition fight with and destroy one another, they fight under the banner, not of Christ, but of the Devil'. Colet also made—with the firm protection of Archbishop Warham—a bold attack on the evil lives of the clergy in the Convocation sermon of 1512. 'Would that for once', he cried, 'you would remember your name and profession and take thought for the reformation of the Church! Never was it more necessary, and never did the state of the Church need more vigorous endeavours. . . . We are troubled by heretics, but no heresy of theirs is so fatal to us and to the people at large as the vicious and depraved lives of the clergy. That is the worst heresy of all.'

The achievements of the new movement of which Colet was so shining an exemplar were not limited to the reform of university teaching by the introduction of Greek studies. Linacre opened up new fields in medicine and was instrumental in founding the Royal College of Physicians, England's first learned society. Colet established St. Paul's School and brought

D

a new impetus to education and a lessening of its brutality; Lily, his high master, wrote a new Latin Grammar. Wolsey founded a new college. Thomas More's lectures on *The City of God* must have formed part of the same programme of enlightenment begun by Grocyn in his Greek lectures at Oxford and continued in mighty sermons in St. Paul's. More's *Utopia* must be accepted as the political programme of the group. And since Erasmus, in part a product of the Oxford at which Grocyn taught, found in Colet a master clothed 'with a dignity and majesty more than human', Erasmus's lifelong labours for European learning may perhaps be added to the accomplishments of the English movement.

More was the youngest of the group of reformers; Grocyn was thirty years his senior, Colet eleven, Linacre eighteen, Lily ten, Erasmus perhaps twelve. With this group of scholars, so much his senior, More became the firmest of friends, and was so closely associated with them that Erasmus wrote in 1499 when More was only twenty-one: 'When I hear my Colet, I seem to be listening to Plato himself. In Grocyn who does not marvel at such a perfect round of learning? What can be more accurate, profound and delicate than the judgment of Linacre? What has nature created more gentle, more sweet, more happy than the genius of Thomas More? I need not go through the list. It is marvellous how general and abundant is the harvest of ancient learning in this country. . . .'

In the same year, as we have already learnt, More presented Erasmus to the nine-year-old Prince Henry: two years later More was to deliver his lectures in St. Lawrence's, in five years to become a Member of Parliament. Everything confirms, in fact, More's youthful brilliance. His genius blossomed early. The boy who went to Oxford as the Lord Chancellor's protégé, prophecies of future greatness preceding him, no doubt, made his impact there at the age of fourteen or fifteen and was certainly counted as a coming man before hurriedly recalled by his father. John More's anxious intervention in his son's career

at the university becomes more understandable if we accept
that it arose because his boy even in his teens attached himself
to the movement founded by Grocyn. John More may well
have shared the suspicions of his generation over the reformation of learning and the introduction of Greek. The Latin that
was good enough for them was good enough for their sons.
John More must have been deeply perturbed lest his impetuous
young son should jeopardize his career by association with
doctrines which might yet be condemned by Church and State.
Or, more humanly, lest the witty and generous boy should
have his head turned by admirers so much older.

The clarion call to reform in Church and State is heard
clearly enough in the voices of Grocyn, Colet, More and the
rest. And Erasmus, it is said, laid the egg which Luther hatched.
And in the years from 1517 to 1522 when Luther's challenge to
the Church was everywhere debated it really was an open
question as to what line Erasmus would take. To many, it must
have seemed that the Reformation was the logical conclusion
of the kind of criticisms which Colet, Erasmus and More had
long been making. More and Erasmus were lifelong friends,
whose joint prestige in the intellectual circles of Europe became immense. In some ways More was England's Erasmus,
and Erasmus was Europe's More. Erasmus became the greatest
European man of letters in More's lifetime—printing made
him a best-seller—and the impact of his enormous output on
the ideas of the time must never be under-estimated. He was a
wit, like More, indeed, the darling wit of Europe; satirist,
Greek scholar, pacifist, and political philosopher; in fact, the
Bernard Shaw and Gilbert Murray of his day. We need therefore to look rather closely at the association of the two men,
and to note both the similarities and the differences between
them, in order that we may learn how much greater More was
than his somewhat irresponsible and elusive literary colleague.

Erasmus, of course, suffered from an obsessive hatred of monks,
and to a lesser extent of priests, and wrote recklessly about

them. The reasons for this are to be sought in his life which he has recorded for us himself in epistles, colloquies, and compendia of one kind or another. Charles Reade, in *Cloister and the Hearth*, that great novel and protestant tract, has made a vivid story of them. Erasmus was born in Rotterdam in 1466 (though there are doubts about this). He was an illegitimate child, almost certainly the son of a priest. But as he tells the story himself his father Gerard, the youngest but one of ten sons of good family, was destined by his parents for the church. Because of that, Gerard kept his intercourse with Margaret, Erasmus's mother, secret. When Gerard found himself bitterly opposed in his desire to marry, he left the country and went to Rome, unaware that Margaret was with child. In Rome he worked as a copyist of books, and his parents falsely sent word to him that Margaret was dead. Overcome with grief Gerard then became a priest, and when he returned home found not only that Margaret was alive, but that he was the father of a small son. It was now impossible for him to marry, but he provided liberally for the boy and in his ninth year the tiny Erasmus went to a school at Deventer, which still exists, and his mother watched over him there. Erasmus reports that the school was barbarous, and though he was speaking of its scholarship, it may have been there that a master broke his heart and made him ill by flogging him, not for any fault the boy had committed, but on grounds that a flogging now and then was good for a boy.

When he was thirteen, this unlucky boy's mother died, and his father prostrated by the news, fell ill and died, too. They were neither much over forty years of age. Erasmus was left in the care of guardians who did not send him to a university, though he was ready for it, but sought to persuade him to enter a monastery. Young Erasmus resisted the pressure, and at that his only active guardian wrote, 'It is all in vain then that I have taken the pains to get such a place for you by great solicitations. You are a scoundrel and under no good influence. I renounce your guardianship. Look out for yourself how to get a living.' To which the reply of the 'scoundrel' was typical: 'Renounce it then, I'm old enough to look after myself.'

The pressure nevertheless did not cease, and ill with fever and sick with uncertainty, he found himself by accident in a house of the Canons Regular at Steyn, near Gouda, and there he met up with an old schoolmate from Deventer for whom he had a violent affection. He took up residence and pursued his studies among the monks with such zest as to influence their love of letters. Somewhat reluctantly, he relates, he made his profession and took priests' orders. By luck he was taken out of the monastery to travel to Rome as the Bishop of Cambrai's secretary. The bishop abandoned the journey but through his patronage Erasmus managed to get sent to Paris, to prosecute his studies at the university. However, 'he shrunk from the study of Theology' (which was why he had been sent there) 'feeling no inclination for it, as he feared he might upset all their foundations, with the result that he should be branded a heretic.' Thenceforth he fought continually to avoid being compelled to return to the loathed monastic life, and for a papal dispensation to relieve him of all the onerous aspects of his vows, such as wearing the habit of his order. And by and large he succeeded, and became Europe's first independent man of letters. There are more versions than one of his life, and by his own hand, and the total effect of them is to persuade us that he entered the monastery at Steyn against his will. Yet his letters of those days do not reveal this, and he was on good terms then with the brother he accused in later life of betraying him into taking the vows. The truth is that Erasmus was neurotic and thin-skinned, a sixteenth-century Rousseau, who could not bear to be under any restraint: for whatever cause he came to hate monastic life, and the fact that he was (fairly certainly) born to Margaret when his father Gerard was already a priest, loaded him with a great grievance against every form of ecclesiastical discipline. He spent much of his life working off that spleen.

# 'A PARLOUS WISE FELLOW'

No more than the rest of his camp was Erasmus able to foresee the tremendous upheaval his own reforming activities were to do so much to bring about. In the period after 1517, rather to his pique, the leadership of the reform movement passed from him to Luther and Melancthon, and he found himself fighting, in the end, and somewhat reluctantly, a rearguard action in defence of the Catholic Church, and of learning, literature and reason against the intolerance and abuse of the Lutherans.

In his own *Compendium of Life*, written in the third person, he said of himself, 'The Lutheran tragedy burdened him with intolerable odium, being torn in pieces by either party, while he tried to benefit both'. Yet part of the Lutheran tragedy was that it was not tragedy enough for him. His faith was of the superficial kind, easily inclining to agnosticism, anticipating in many ways the rationalism of the eighteenth-century Enlightenment; to the meaning of Luther's passionate and rock-like obstinacy Erasmus had no clue. Religious feeling of such intensity struck no answering chord in him. He would have been quite incapable of the unswerving resolution of Thomas More.

Yet it remains sadly true that Erasmus, by his satirical attacks on the Church, laid the egg which Luther hatched, and for a long time Erasmus sought to ingratiate himself with both sides to the controversy over Luther's theses and subsequent acts of justification, by judicious letters of flattery. His behaviour was notoriously shifty, too; he spread the rumour that Leo X's bull against Luther was a forgery and so helped to screen Luther at an extremely critical moment. And when the Elector Frederick of Saxony enquired of Erasmus, in the month that Luther burnt the papal bull, what he thought of the man, Erasmus in effect came down heavily on Luther's side. Erasmus, the greatest man of learning in Europe, hummed and haahed, puffed his cheeks and smacked his lips and gave birth to the irresponsible epigram which was presently racing through Germany. 'Luther', he said, 'has sinned in two things: namely, because he has

touched the Pontiff's crown and the monks' bellies.' The vanity
of Erasmus is plainly to be discerned in such silliness. After this
judgment it was hardly likely that Elector Frederick would
seek to restrain Luther, or to withdraw his protection. When
Erasmus ultimately was persuaded to write and speak against
the Lutherans, he did so with great effectiveness (notably in *De
Libero Arbitrio*), but too late to heal the wound opening across
the body of Europe.

It seems to have been in the summer of 1499 that Lord
Mountjoy, first the pupil of Erasmus, and later his 'Maecenas',
brought him to England. There is a silly story that More and
Erasmus first met at the Lord Mayor's table and having exchanged repartees in Latin, Erasmus said, *Aut tu es Morus aut
nullus* (You are More or no one), to which More retorted, *Et
tu es aut Deus, aut demon, aut meus Erasmus* (You are either God,
the Devil, or my own Erasmus). In the Elizabethan play, *Sir
Thomas More*, an even sillier version of the meeting is cooked
up, for in that More is supposed to dress up his servant Randal
in the chancellor's robes and sit him in state to receive Erasmus,
who is naturally surprised to be greeted by a Lord Chancellor
who exclaims, 'Wilt supp with me? By God, I love a parlous
wise fellow that smells of a pollititian better than a long progress', and goes on to ask, 'How longe will a Holland cheese in
your countrie keepe without maggetts?'

What happened, indeed, at their earliest meeting, or how it
took place, we do not know. But the English humanists—
More, Grocyn, Colet, Linacre, Lily—will not have been tardy
in arranging to meet the not unknown scholar, vouched for by
Lord Mountjoy, his pupil and friend. And of the earliest recorded association with More what could have been more
momentous than that they should go together, from Lord
Mountjoy's house near Greenwich, to visit the royal children
at Eltham Palace?

'I was staying at lord Mountjoy's country house when
Thomas More came to see me,' Erasmus wrote, 'and took me

out with him for a walk as far as the next village, where all
the king's children, except prince Arthur, who was then the
eldest son, were being educated. When we came into the hall,
the attendants not only of the palace but also of Mountjoy's
household were all assembled. In the midst stood prince Henry,
then nine years old, and having already something of royalty
in his demeanour, in which there was a certain dignity combined with singular courtesy. On his right was Margaret, about
eleven years of age, afterwards married to James, king of Scots;
and on his left played Mary, a child of four. Edmund was an
infant in arms. More, with his companion Arnold, after paying
his respects to the boy Henry, the same that is now king of
England, presented him with some writing. For my part, not
having expected anything of the sort, I had nothing to offer,
but promised that on another occasion I would in some way
declare my duty towards him. Meantime I was angry with
More for not having warned me, especially as the boy sent me
a little note, while we were at dinner, to challenge something
from my pen. I went home, and in the Muses' spite, from whom
I had been so long divorced, finished the poem within three
days.'

The presence of Lord Mountjoy's retinue at Eltham Palace
gives the whole game away: he and More had contrived this
meeting so that Erasmus might be confronted with the prince
they hoped would become his patron. True, Henry was not
then heir to the throne, but that he was destined for the Church
makes the meeting still more important, for a prince of the
Church would have been a European, not simply an English
patron of the letters of Erasmus.

Erasmus fell in love with England and in 1499 wrote to
Robert Fisher in Italy: 'But how do you like our England, you
will say. Believe me, my Robert, when I answer that I never
liked anything so much before. I find the climate both pleasant
and wholesome, and so much learning, not hackneyed and trivial
but deep, accurate, ancient, Latin and Greek, that but for the

curiosity of seeing it, I do not now so much care for Italy.' He then goes on to make those praises of Colet, Grocyn, Linacre and More which I have already quoted. In another letter of the same year he boasted that in England he had become almost a sportsman, no bad rider, and a practised courtier who bows and smiles with grace. He urged his correspondent to take his snout out of the French filth, send his gout to the devil, and fly to England. 'To take one attraction of many; there are nymphs here with divine features, so gentle and kind, that you may well prefer them to your Camenae. Besides, there is a fashion which cannot be commended enough. Wherever you go, you are received on all hands with kisses; when you take your leave, you are dismissed with kisses. If you go back your salutes are returned to you. When a visit is paid, the first act of hospitality is a kiss, and when guests depart, the same entertainment is repeated; wherever a meeting takes place there is kissing in abundance; in fact whatever way you turn, you are never without it. Oh Faustus, if you had once tasted how sweet and fragrant those kisses are, you would indeed wish to be a traveller, not for ten years, like Solon, but for your whole life, in England.'

The links made by Erasmus in England lasted a lifetime. The Oxford scholars, first his teachers, were soon his allies and supporters. The learned Archbishop Warham gave Erasmus his patronage, and it was with Colet that he rowed up to Lambeth Palace to meet him. Eventually Erasmus was awarded the absentee living of Aldington in Kent, which he was somewhat reluctant to take, having condemned this kind of thing many times himself. The archbishop is said to have replied to his hesitation, 'Who has a fairer claim to live out of a church income than you, the one person who by your valuable writings instructs and educates the parsons themselves, and indeed all the churches of the world?'

We cannot trace the whole of Erasmus's career. But he remained constantly in touch with More and his circle, and corresponded vigorously with them all. He lectured in Greek at Cambridge. He stayed with More in Bucklersbury, and there wrote his masterpiece, *In Praise of Folly*, and More, on his part, followed with the closest attention the work of Erasmus and took his side in the controversies in which he was so often engaged, and met him when he went abroad on embassies. Their mutual love and admiration suffered no check. When Erasmus was attacked More proclaimed that he was the dearest friend that he had: 'Erasmus has published volumes more full of wisdom that Europe has seen for ages.' And when More was executed, Erasmus, an old man already, felt that he had died himself. 'We had but one soul between us.' He lamented his vanished friends of a golden age in these terms, 'First William Warham, Archbishop of Canterbury, then of late Mountjoy, and Fisher of Rochester, and Thomas More, Lord Chancellor of England, whose soul was more pure than any snow, whose genius was such as England never had—yea, and never shall again, mother of good wits though England be.' Erasmus then was worn out; the cardinal's hat offered to him in 1534 had held no attractions; he was incapable of a new start and died a year later than More of a return of the dysentery from which he had often suffered.

There are many eulogies of More in the letters of Erasmus. With some of them we are already acquainted. More was always the man 'whose eloquence . . . is such that he could persuade even an enemy to do whatever he pleased, while my own affection for the man is so great, that if he bade me dance a hornpipe, I should do at once just as he bade me.' And our picture of More as he was seen by his illustrious contemporary would be incomplete without extracts from the famous letter to Ulrich von Hutten. In it we find a portrait of the physical More:

'To begin with that part of him which is least known to you —in shape and stature More is not a tall man, but not remarkably short, all his limbs being so symmetrical, that no deficiency is observed in this respect. His complexion is fair, being blonde rather than pale, but with no approach to redness, except a very delicate flush, which lights up the whole. His hair is auburn inclining to black, or if you like it better, black inclining to auburn; his beard thin, his eyes a bluish grey with some sort of tinting upon them. This kind of eye is thought to be a sign of the happiest character, and is regarded with favour in England, whereas with us black eyes are rather preferred. It is said, that no kind of eye is so free from defects of sight. His countenance answers for his character, having an expression of kind and friendly cheerfulness with a little air of raillery. To speak candidly, it is a face more expressive of pleasantry than of gravity or dignity, though very far removed from folly or buffoonery. His right shoulder seems a little higher than his left, especially when he is walking, a peculiarity that is not innate, but the result of habit, like many tricks of the kind. In the rest of his body there is nothing displeasing, only his hands are a little coarse, or appear so, as compared with the rest of his figure. He has always been very negligent of his toilet, so as not to give much attention even to the things which according to Ovid are all that men care about. What a charm there was in his looks when young, may even now be inferred from what remains; although I knew him myself when he was not more than three-and-twenty years old; for he has not yet passed his fortieth year. . . . His voice is neither loud nor excessively low, but of a penetrating tone. It has nothing in it melodious or soft, but is simply suitable for speech, as it does not seem to have any natural talent for singing, though he takes pleasure in music of every kind. His articulation is wonderfully distinct, being equally free from hurry and from hesitation.'[3]

Erasmus goes on to relate that More likes to dress simply, and cares little for all the formalities of daily life, and that he regards the courtly trifles on which so many waste their days 'effeminate'. He was therefore reluctant to be drawn into court life, the more as he had 'a special hatred for tyranny and a great fancy for equality'.

'He seems to be born and made for friendship, of which he is
the sincerest and most persistent devotee. Neither is he afraid
of that multiplicity of friends, of which Hesiod disapproves.
Accessible to every tender of intimacy, he is by no means
fastidious in choosing his acquaintance, while he is most accom-
modating in keeping it on foot, and constant in retaining it. If
he has fallen in with anyone whose faults he cannot cure, he
finds some opportunity of parting with him, untying the knot
of intimacy without tearing it.'[4]

In short, he is the perfect friend; moreover, a most witty one,
'from boyhood . . . so pleased with a joke, that it might seem
that jesting was the main object of his life. . . . When quite a
youth, he wrote farces and acted them. If a thing was faceti-
ously said, even though it was aimed at himself, he was
charmed with it, so much did he enjoy any witticism that had a
flavour of subtlety or genius. This led to his amusing himself
as a young man with epigrams, and taking great delight in
Lucian. Indeed, it was he that suggested my writing the *Moria*,
or *Praise of Folly*, which was much the same thing as setting a
camel to dance.'[5]

More is a second Democritus, or else 'that Pythagorean
philosopher, who strolls in leisurely mood through the market-
place, contemplating the turmoil of those who buy and sell'.
Yet more than that, 'he is a steady adherent of true piety;
having regular hours for his prayers, which are not uttered by
rote, but from the heart. He talks with his friends about a
future life in such a way as to make you feel that he believes
what he says, and does not speak without the best hope. Such is
More, even at Court; and there are still people who think that
Christians are only to be found in monasteries.'[6]

If the praise of More is sometimes fulsome, it reflects nevertheless a real intimacy, and Erasmus meant what he said when
he spoke of their common soul. But how far were they really
of one *mind*? This is an extremely important question in the
light of More's martyrdom for his faith. Was he the defender of

the faith, or the reformer who failed to go far enough? Was he of one mind about the Church when he was young, and another when he was old? Was he another who, a revolutionary in his youth, swung to reaction when the fires died down? Was he, so to speak, a Protestant whose nerve failed him?

*Moriae Encomium*, or *Praise of Folly*, deliberately puns upon More's name in the title, and is dedicated to him in terms which identify him with the book. The epistle to More says: 'Having resolved to be a doing, and deeming that time improper for any serious concerns, I thought good to divert myself with drawing up a panegyrick upon Folly. How! what maggot (say you) put this in your head? why, the first hint, Sir, was your own surname More, which comes as near the literal sound of the word Μωρία as you yourself are the distant signification of it, and that in all men's judgments is vastly wide. In the next place I supposed that this kind of sporting wit would be more especially accepted by you, Sir, who are wont with this sort of jocose raillery (such as I mistake not is neither dull nor impertinent) to be mightily pleased. . . . I hope therefore you will not only readily accept of this rude essay as a token from your friend, but take it under your immediate protection, as being dedicated to you, and by that title adopted for yours, rather than be fathered as my own.'⁷

Obviously, Erasmus felt that the book bore the imprint of both their minds, and not only from its having been written in More's house. At the very least he was certain it would bring pleasure to his friend. But 'jocose raillery' it is not, but the most devastating criticism of much that went on in his own day. The attacks on dice-players, cuckolds, schoolmasters (already quoted), philosophers, vain and ambitious monarchs, might have been made in any age on precisely such kinds of men, though seldom as wittily, and are of no particular significance for our argument, but the showing up of church scandals was something with the most pointed contemporary application. One must suppose that there had long been fools who made 'a trade of telling or enquiring after incredible stories, of miracles or prodigies . . . and such others as attribute strange virtues to the shrines and images of saints and martyrs', but the sale of indulgences was a growing corruption, attacked with pure wrath: 'By this easy way of purchasing pardons, any notorious highwayman, and plundering soldier, or any bribe-taking judge, shall disburse some part of their unjust gains, and so think all their grossest impieties sufficiently atoned for; so many perjuries, lusts, drunkennesses, quarrels, bloodsheds, treats, treacheries, and all sorts of debaucheries, shall all be, as it were, struck a bargain for, and such a contract made as if they had paid off all arrears, and might now begin upon a new score.'[8]

The rise of Mariolatry is attacked in these terms, 'There are some more catholic saints, petitioned upon all occasions, as more especially the Virgin Mary, whose blind devotees think it manners now to place the mother before the Son.' Priests are spoken of with contempt, 'Almost all christians being wretch-edly enslaved to blindness and ignorance, which the priests are so far from preventing or removing, that they blacken the darkness, and promote the delusion, wisely foreseeing that the people( like cows, which never give down their milk so well as when they are gently stroaked) would part with less if they knew more.'[9] While as for the Popes, if they did but for one moment remember that they were followers of Christ, com-mitted by their role as Christ's vicars to lead his life of preach-ing and poverty, then, 'There would be no such vigorous making of parties, and buying of votes in the conclave, upon a vacancy of that see; and those who by bribery, or other in-direct courses, should get themselves elected, would never secure their sitting firm in the chair by pistol, poison, force, and violence.'[10]

Many of the *Colloquies* of Erasmus pursue the same kind of exposure of monkish or priestly greed and dishonesty, or of popular superstitions. To one, *The Religious Pilgrimage*, wherein the commercialization of the shrines of Walsingham and Canterbury is satirized with relish, I have already drawn attention. As for the attacks on monks in books and epistles, they are too numerous to mention.

Erasmus's *Enchiridion Militis Christiani*—his handbook for a Christian knight—rubbed home in a scholarly way the lessons of his satirical works; 'it was not', he explained to Colet, 'composed for any display of genius or eloquence, but only for the purpose of correcting the common error of those who make religion consist of ceremonies and an almost more than Jewish observance of corporeal matters, while they are singularly careless of things that belong to piety. I have endeavoured nevertheless to lay down a sort of Art of Piety, after the manner of those who have composed systems of instruction in various branches of knowledge.'

It can be understood why Erasmus was often attacked in his day. The monks were specially apt to return his abuse. One monk addressed a letter to Thomas More urging him to sever his association with this heretical foreigner. More made a powerful defence of his friend. Amongst other matters, More suggested in his epistle that the saints and fathers of the church had not believed in the immaculate conception of the Virgin Mary; and, against Mariolatry, the counter-attack of More was as vigorous as anything Erasmus himself could have launched. Do not the orders, he asked, quarrel and abuse each other, and fight over the cut and colour of their gowns? Yet the same men who will think themselves damned if they change the shape of their frocks, will intrigue and lie. Though they shudder if they find they have left out the verse of a Psalm, they tell each other dirty stories longer than their prayers. They fancy themselves the holiest of men and commit the most abominable crimes. And then More goes on to relate the story of the prior of a strict house who had gone from wickedness to wickedness and finally planned murder and sacrilege. The prior hired a party of cut-throats to do the deed. The men were caught, and seen by

More, and they confessed. 'They told me themselves', he relates, 'that before they went to work the prior took them to his cell and made them pray on their knees to the Virgin there. This completed, they did their business with a clear conscience.'

In this same letter he spoke, against Mariolatry, of a certain Franciscan monk at Coventry who had been preaching to the people that whoever read daily through the Psalter of the blessed Virgin could never be damned. More's judgment of this had been sought and he had pointed out that no earthly prince would be so foolish as to forgive rebellion against him simply on the grounds that those who had attempted it had sought to exculpate their crimes by paying reverence to his mother!

In many of his epigrams More shows the same anti-clerical spirit as Erasmus. His jest of the crew which threw the monk overboard is well known through Archdeacon Wrangham's translation:

> *A squall arose; the vessel's tossed;*
> *The sailors fear their lives are lost.*
> *Our sins, our sins,—dismayed they cry,*
> *Have wrought this fatal destiny.*

> *A monk it chanced was of the crew,*
> *And round him to confess they drew.*
> *Yet still the restless ship is tossed,*
> *And still they fear their lives are lost.*

> *One sailor, keener than the rest,*
> *Cries—with our sins she's still oppressed;*
> *Heave out that monk, who bears them all,*
> *And then full well she'll ride the squall.*

*So said, so done:—with one accord*
*They throw the caitiff overboard.*
*And now the bark before the gale*
*Scuds with light hull and easy sail.*

*Learn hence the weight of sin to know,*
*With which a ship could hardly go.*

More venomous was an epigram against the appointment of
a certain priest to a living. Thomas More was, in fact, particularly the opponent of indiscriminate ordination, and his account
of the priesthood of Utopia, which consisted of very holy men,
*and therefore very few*, is designed to make this criticism with
greater effect than he could do in his Latin epigrams. The epigram congratulates the flock on their new pastor: 'Unless I
am blinded by partiality, it would be almost impossible to find
another like him. Without a spark of that useless learning
which serves only to puff up its possessor with pride, he is endowed with such a combination of rare virtues as could scarcely
be equalled even among the ancient fathers of the Church. He
shows in his own conduct, as in a glass, what his people ought
to do, and what leave undone; all they require being a simple
admonition to *practise* whatever they see him avoid, and to *avoid*
everything which he *practises*.'[11]

More showed his detestation of the impurities of the Church
by the preface he wrote (as a dedicatory epistle to Dr. Thomas
Ruthall, the King's secretary) in 1506, to his translations of
Lucian's dialogues. He said, 'No wonder then, if ruder minds
are affected by the fictions of those who think they have done
a lasting service to Christ, when they have invented a fable
about some saint, or a tragic description of Hell, which either
melts an old woman to tears, or makes her blood run cold.
There is scarcely any life of a Martyr or Virgin, in which some
falsehood of this kind has not been inserted; an act of piety no
doubt, considering the risk that Truth would be insufficient,

E                                    65

unless propped up by lies! Thus they have not scrupled to stain with fiction that Religion, which was founded by Truth herself, and ought to consist of naked truth. They have failed to see, that such fables are so far from aiding religion, that nothing can be more injurious to it. It is obvious, as Augustine himself has observed, that where there is any scent of a lie, the authority of truth is immediately weakened and destroyed. . . . Therefore while the histories commended to us by divinely inspired Scripture ought to be accepted with undoubting faith, the others, tested by the doctrine of Christ, as by the rule of Critolaus, should either be received with caution or rejected. . . .'

More's choice of literary heroes was significant, too, for after Plato came the mocking Lucian, and after him, Pico della Mirandola, whose life he wrote in 1510, and who was hardly a model of orthodoxy.

More confessed that in his youth he thought of the papacy as something of a man-made institution, and though he changed his mind as the years went by, in 1532, in his controversy with Tyndale he placed the General Council above the Pope, with power to depose him. When attacked upon the ground that he had provoked Henry VIII to set forth arguments in favour of the Pope's authority which had put a sword in the hands of the Pope against the King, he replied that he had taken the opposite course, reminding the King that the Pope was a prince as he was, and that it would be better if the matter of his authority were more lightly touched upon lest it should be used against the King in any breach between them.

Here, then, was no conventional Christian echoing the phrases of others, but one who exercised his luminous intelligence above all on his faith: nothing escaped his critical examination, and it is not, as with Erasmus, agnosticism which makes him scornful of superstition and corruption, but a faith as warm as Colet's. More was too profoundly religious to be embittered. Erasmus hated the monastic system and suspected all priests and was forever running away from ecclesiasticism.

More was empty of the hatreds which possessed his friend. He had abandoned the monastic life, not with joy but with reluctance, and all his life he respected those who found it in them to take monastic vows. Into the secular life he imported the disciplines of the monastery, and his lonely preparation for death was as stern as any which might have taken place within monastery walls. His contempt of bad priests and ecclesiastical corruption came not from that impatience with, or resentment of, the religious or priestly life which possessed so many Tudors, but from exactly the opposite, from an anger that something so infinitely precious should be ruined by the evil of some men. He was like the critic who sees a good play badly acted, and condemns the actors while he acclaims the play.

In *The Apology* he wrote after his resignation from the Chancellorship we meet, not the young scholar and wit, but a man matured by years of experience in religious controversy and a statesman but recently responsible for the safety of the realm. I am not so much of a poet, he explains, as Tyndale and Frith have called me, 'as to find good names for evil things' and can not 'call a fool but a fool, nor a heretic but a heretic'. Are we to say, he asks, that Christians have been living in idolatry these eight hundred years, and dying in the service of the Devil 'because they have done honour to Christ's Cross, and prayed unto the saints, and reverenced their relics, and honoured their images, and been baptized in Latin, and taken matrimony for a sacrament, and used confession and done penance for sins, and prayed for all Christian souls, and been anealed in their deathbed, and have taken their housel after the rite and usage of the Church, and have set more by the Mass than they should do, and believed it was a sacrifice, a host, and an oblation, and that it should do them good; and have believed that there was neither bread nor wine in the Blessed Sacrament of the altar, but instead of bread and wine the very Body and Blood of Christ'.[12]

We can understand, from that tremendous defence, that

More wanted this said of him, 'My epitaph shall record that I have been an enemy to heretics. I say it deliberately, I do so detest that class of men that unless they repent I am the worst enemy they have.' Let us be charitable, however, and say that the same conflict with heresy brought Erasmus to his side in the end, in defence of the faith in which Erasmus, too, had been trained.

# CHAPTER FOUR

# THE LONDONER

The year 1505, in which More translated Lucian's Dialogues, was marked by an event more obviously connected with his decision that he was not a fit candidate
for monastic life: his marriage to Jane Colt. Roper's *Life* simply
relates that More lived without vow for about four years with
the London Carthusians '*until* he resorted to the house of one
Mr. Colt, a gentleman of Essex that had oft invited him thither,
having three daughters whose honest conversation and virtuous
education provoked him there especially to set his affection'.
What he then tells us is very typical of More: 'And albeit his
mind most served him to the second daughter, for that he
thought her the fairest and best favoured, yet when he considered that it would be both great grief and some shame also
to the eldest to see her younger sister in marriage preferred before her, he then of a certain pity framed his fancy towards her,
and soon after married her, nevertheless not discontinuing his
study of the law at Lincoln's Inn, but applying still the same
until he was called to the Bench, and had read twice, which is
as often as any judge of the law doth read.'

He established his wife, a girl of seventeen, in his house at
Bucklersbury, and the pair of them were perhaps unfortunate
to be so shrewdly observed by Erasmus, who visited them soon
after—if the colloquy, *The Uneasy Wife*, is to be trusted as a
picture of their relationship. In the famous letter to von
Hutten we find this: 'When he married, he chose a very young
girl, a lady by birth with her character still unformed, having

been always kept in the country with her parents and sisters—
so that he was all the better able to fashion her according to his
own habits. Under his direction she was instructed in learning
and in every kind of music, and had almost completely become
just such a person as would have been a delightful companion
for his whole life, if an early death had not carried her away.'
Jane's first child was born in December 1505, the Margaret who
cleaved so staunchly to her father throughout his life, and if
Jane is to be judged by her first-born, what a fine person she
must have been! The charming Jane, 'chara uxorcula', as he
called her in the epitaph that he composed for his own monument, bore him two other daughters, Elizabeth and Cecilia.
Son John was born in 1509, but in the following year Jane died.
Before many months were out, against the advice of his friends,
More married again, this time a widow, Alice Middleton,
whose first husband had been a merchant of the Staple of
Calais. More had four very young children and desperately
needed someone to care for them, and this, Dame Alice, who
bore him no children of her own, seems to have done to every-
one's satisfaction.

Erasmus gives this account of her: 'She is no great beauty,
nor yet young, *nec bella admodum nec puella*, as he [More] sometimes says, but a sharp and watchful housewife; with whom
nevertheless he lives, on as sweet and pleasant terms as if she
were as young and lovely as anyone could desire; and scarcely
any husband obtains from his wife by masterfulness and severity as much compliance as he does by blandishments and jests.
Indeed, what more compliance could he have, when he has
induced a woman who is already elderly, who is not naturally
of a yielding character, and whose mind is occupied with
business, to learn to play the harp, the viol, the spinet and the
flute, and to give up every day a prescribed time to practice.
With similar kindness he rules his whole household, in which
there are no tragic incidents, and no quarrels. If anything of the
kind should be likely, he either calms it down or applies a

remedy at once. And in parting with any member of his household he has never acted in a hostile spirit, or treated him as an enemy. Indeed his house seems to have a fatal felicity, no one having lived in it without being advanced to higher fortune, no inmate ever having had a stain upon his character.'[1]

This is high praise indeed for any household, and the more remarkable tribute to Thomas More's grace and understanding since his first marriage was the result of a certain pity, and his second the quickest way of getting a competent housekeeper. It reveals what we shall meet again and again, how highly More valued people for themselves, and to what endless sacrifice he was prepared to go to honour their personal demands upon him. Erasmus was not always so gracious concerning Dame Alice, and did not always get on with her, and he, in his turn, with his delicate stomach, his fastidiousness, and his lack of English must equally have been a trial to her. And Ammonio, the Italian scholar who became Latin secretary to Henry VIII, and who for a time resided in More's house, spoke of himself as happy to have left it since he no longer sees 'the hooked beak of the harpy'.

Poor, unlovely Alice was no scholar; her world was not Thomas More's world, and she never understood his genius or his scruples of conscience. To the end she could not understand why he, her famous husband, did not do what the other gentlemen did to please the King, and so keep his station with the best of them. Even in the matter of the hair shirt she was not admitted to her husband's confidence, and 'marvelled where his shirts were washed' and was reduced to complaining to More's father-confessor about the matter when she finally learnt what he wore to 'tame his flesh'. Was she a shrew? Indeed, she may have been, but if so not of the malicious kind, but of that bustling, practical sort, whose shrewishness is a bantering impatience with the absurdities of men, who will forever make complicated what is patently simple. Shakespeare knew her sort. And all the evidence points to the fact that she was a foil for More's own ready tongue, and knew it, and they got along very well together as a consequence. She could, in any case, no more resist this charmer than the rest of her contemporaries.

She was a Londoner, and More understood and loved Londoners; he possessed their shrewdness, their worldly good sense, and was very much their representative man. To see More in the round we must see him against the background to which Dame Alice also belonged. This London scholar, barrister, civil servant, statesman, was the first layman to hold the office of Lord Chancellor, and was without compensation of noble birth. His independence of mind and bearing, however, are not the less but the more for his origins, and we never feel that he is a promoted underling, but rather one naturally born to power. We have already discovered that he despised ornate and flowery civilities, had no interest in magnificent clothes, no ambitions of a courtly kind and was drawn into the King's service against his will. Indeed, upon his entry into the King's service, he read his monarch a long lecture, *Utopia*, that the King might understand what manner of man he was employing!

He was so sure of himself that we are entitled to ask the origin of this independence and manliness. If *bourgeois* were not an overworked Marxist epithet one might proudly apply it to him. He was of the new middle class created by London trade and enterprise, a man independent of the monarchy and nobility by birth and upbringing, and neither hostile to the nobly born, nor subservient.

Erasmus spoke of him as inclining towards equality, and More's *Epigrammata* reveals that he shared many of the suspicions of the burgesses about princes, and numerous shafts are directed against kings and tyrants. One epigram tells, for instance, the story of a rustic who joins a crowd waiting to see the King ride by and then finds to his surprise that he is nothing but a man in fine clothes riding a horse, a tale which reminds one of the Hans Andersen story of the King who wore no clothes. When the King, with 'sumptuous train . . . bedecked with glittering gold' pranced along on his 'comely courser'

> '*The King—the King—O where is he?*'—
>   *The clown began to cry:*
> *Quoth one, with finger pointed out,*—
>   '*Lo where he sits on high!*'
>
> '*Tush, that is not the King*,' *quoth he*—
>   '*Thou art deceived quite.*
> '*That seemeth but a man to me,*
>   '*In painted vesture dight.*'[2]

Far more serious in its implications is the epigram 'A Tyrant in sleep differeth not from a common person', which is Shakespearian in its savagery. Here is a translation:

> *Does therefore swell and pout with pride*
>   *And rear thy snout on high,*
> *Because the crowd doth crowd and couch*
>   *Whereso thou comest by:*
> *Because the people bonnet-less*
>   *Before thee still do stand;*
> *Because the life and death doth lie*
>   *Of divers in thy hand?*
> *But when that drowsy sleep of thee*
>   *Hath every part possessed,*
> *Tell then where is thy pomp and pride,*
>   *Thy porte and all the rest?*
> *Then, snorting lozzel as thou art,*
>   *Thou liest like a block;*
> *Or as a carrion corpse late dead,*
>   *As senseless as a stock.*
> *And if it were not that thou wert*
>   *Closed up in walls of stone,*
> *And fenced around—thy life would be*
>   *In hands of every one.*[3]

In these and other epigrams which reveal what we are in-clined to describe as republican and tyrannicidal feelings, we glimpse the proud and fiery spirit normally hidden by More's self-control, and we can see why his contemporaries thought of him as an obstinate man. More's self-discipline is so great, his charity so boundless, that we are tempted to convert him into a spirit all sweetness and light, torn from his books and family to a martyrdom the more poignant because so undeserved. But we forget More's iron will; it is this which supports his gracious life through all its trials. It was the equal of Henry VIII's or Luther's, though not so well-equipped as theirs with temporal power. No man knew better than Henry VIII what the failure to bend that will would mean to his prestige in the matter of the divorce and the supremacy. That was why Henry determined to destroy his ex-Chancellor. If we are prone to overlook More's strong will it is because it was never self-will as Henry's almost always was, nor self-indulgence, like Wolsey's, but a will obedient to a high morality and a keen intellect.

In More's first encounter with princes his will was matched against theirs. This carries us back to that remarkable opening to his public career when, in the year before his marriage to Jane Colt, he became a Member of Parliament and even, young though he was, its leader. As Roper tells the story, More, 'who ere ever he had been reader in Court was in the latter time of King Henry the Seventh made a Burgess in Parliament, where-in there were by the King demanded (as I have heard it re-ported) about three-fifteenths for the marriage of his eldest daughter, that then should be the Scottish Queen. At the last debating whereof he [More] made such arguments and reasons there against, that the King's demands were thereby overthrown. So that one of the King's privy chamber, named Mr. Tyler, being present thereat, brought word to the King out of the Parliament house, that a beardless boy had dis-appointed all his purposes. Whereupon the King conceiving

74

great indignation towards him could not be satisfied until he had some way revenged it.'

It was difficult to throw a Burgess of Parliament into jail for this offence without raising widespread resentment in the country and uneasiness among the other burgesses concerning their parliamentary immunity. Roper tells us that More was too poor to be worth prosecuting, and 'forasmuch as he nothing having, nothing could lose, his grace devised a causeless quarrel against his father, keeping him in the Tower until he had paid him an hundred pounds fine'. It is a pity John More's blistering comments about this episode are lost to history. Perhaps it made him regret having made a lawyer of young Thomas; as a cleric he might have been out of harm's way.

The impertinence of Thomas so worked up the enmity of the King and his council towards him that for a time it looked as if his life might be in danger. According to Roper, when Thomas More saw Dr. Fox, Bishop of Winchester, Privy Councillor, and one of the King's closest advisers, soon after, Fox 'called him aside, and pretended great favour towards him [and] promised him that if he would be ruled by him, he would not fail but into the King's favour again to restore him'. This was taken by More's friends to mean that Fox was urging him to confess to a fault against the King, and that once such a confession was made, it would be easier for the King to take direct action to punish him. Moreover, one friend said, Bishop Fox 'to serve the King's turn will not stick to agree to his own father's death'.

More kept out of the trap, and even considered going abroad, and his most bitter epigrams against kings and tyrants date from these years. The trouble with the King was a great trial to him, and it was with relief that he welcomed the accession of Henry VIII in 1509.

More's London patriotism reveals itself very strongly in his *Richard the Third*, for London's role in the usurpation was an obvious one; by appealing to the liberties of its citizens

Richard hoped to hold fast to the throne. For London was, of course, the maker and breaker of princes, and it was, for instance, London's decision which ruined Margaret of Anjou in her struggle for the throne. Nothing throws more light on Thomas More's understanding of the king-making role of Londoners than his account of the efforts of the Protector, Richard Duke of Gloucester, to win London citizens to his side in 1483. Thomas was five years old then, a precocious boy beyond a doubt, and able to recall something of the atmosphere of that dark year, and to have reconstructed much more from the talk in his father's, and in Archbishop Morton's, households. Take, for example, the sermon preached by Dr. Shaw at Paul's cross, which was intended to establish Richard's claims by hinting that the princes in the Tower were bastards. In his brilliant history, More's account of it has an eye-witness's vividness. It was arranged, More tells us, that as the preacher was extolling the virtues of the Protector, he, Richard, should stroll among the people who, it was expected, would then, with a little prompting, cry out 'King Richard! King Richard!' like any pack of rustic idiots. But the timing went wrong, and the preacher reached that part of his sermon before Richard appeared, and had perforce to go back again, and throw the cues at the people for a second time; even so, 'the people were so far from crying "King Richard!" that they stood as they had been turned into stones, for wonder of this shameful sermon. After which once ended, the preacher got him home and never after durst look out for shame but keep him out of sight like an owl.' Was John More at Paul's Cross, with his little son perched on his shoulder? He could have been, but must certainly have been at the Guildhall (without Thomas) 'on the Tuesday after' when the Duke of Buckingham, men-at-arms clashing around him, made his subtle speech to the commons of the city, in which he craftily peddled the Protector's claim to the throne by blackening every other claimant to it. 'When the Duke had said, and looked that the people, whom he had hoped the Mayor had framed before, should after this proposition made, have cried "King Richard! King Richard!" —all was hushed and mute and not one word answered thereunto.

' "What meaneth this, that this people be so still?"

' "Sir," quoth the Mayor, "percase they perceive you not well."

' "That we shall mend," quoth he, "if that will help." '

And he tried again, more loudly, to win over the citizenry. But still they stood in 'a marvellous obstinate silence'. Then at a third attempt to persuade them to answer whether or not they would have Richard as king, the people simply whispered furiously among themselves 'as it were the sound of a swarm of bees'. And when some prentice boys burst into the back of the hall and threw up their caps and shouted, 'King Richard! King Richard!' those in front of them turned their heads in astonishment, but still said nothing. The Duke took this as a plebiscite, but among the citizens, at all this roguery, 'the dolour of their hearts burst out at their eyes'.

*The History of Richard the Third*, which was published in 1513, was not written against royalty, but it is quite without illusions about it, and the pride of More in the behaviour of most of the citizens of London is as plain as a pikestaff.

There were certain other incidents in More's life which demonstrated the importance of his status in the city. In September 1510 he was appointed Under-Sheriff of London. This legal position is described by Erasmus in these terms: 'In the City of London, where he was born, he acted for some years as judge in civil causes. This office, which is by no means burdensome—inasmuch as the Court sits only on Thursdays before dinner—is considered highly honourable; and no judge ever disposed of more suits, or conducted himself with more perfect integrity. In most cases he remitted the fees which are due from the litigants, the practice being for the plaintiff to deposit three groats before the hearing, and the defendant a like sum, and no more being allowed to be exacted. By such conduct he made himself extremely popular in the City.' His record in this office accords with what we are told of the rectitude of his law practice—that he would seek to persuade his clients to come to terms, and to avoid the expense of litigation, but if they must go to law, then to show them what was the cheapest way.

In 1517 the London mob broke out in riots against foreigners which earned for the May Day of that year the title 'Evil May Day', and so it has come down in ballad and story. Hall's *Chronicles* tell how in the eighth year of Henry's reign the citizens of London, more especially the prentices and journeymen, began to grow restless about the number and insolence of foreigners in the city. It was popularly alleged that their presence was depriving 'the poore Englishe artificers' of the means of getting a living, and was the cause of scarcity and high prices in the markets. There were some scandals, such as that the servant of an ambassador took out of the hands of a carpenter two stockdoves he had bought for the pot, and carried them off to the embassy, refusing even to reimburse the carpenter what he had paid for them. Worse, a Lombard had not only enticed a man's wife to his house, but actually sued her husband for her board and lodging!

An ill-advised preacher at Saint Mary Spital preached a sermon against foreigners, and almost on the eve of May Day, after some unorganized assaults on foreigners, the rumour went round that 'on May daye next, the citie would rebell, and slaye all aliens'. Even the King heard this, in his court at Richmond, and sent for the Mayor, who (seeming to be the only man who had not heard the rumour) gave Wolsey assurances that the city was quiet and the King's peace would be observed. The city council enlightened the Mayor, and he and the council, with the Cardinal's consent, proclaimed a curfew—'that every man should repair to his own house, and there to keep him and his servants till vii. of the clock of the morning: with which commandment the said Richard Brooke, sergeant at the law, and Sir Thomas More, late under-sheriff of London, and then of the king's council, came to the Guild Hall half an hour before ix. of the clock, and there shewed the commandment of the king's council. Then all in haste every alderman sent to his ward, that no man should stir after ix. of the clock out of his house, but to kepe his doors shut and his servants within till vii. of the clock in the morning. After this commandment, Sir John Munday, alderman, came from his ward, and found two young men in Chepe playing at bucklers, and a great company of young men looking on them, for the commandment was then scarce known, for it was then but ix. of the clock. Master Munday seeing that, bade them leave; and the one young man asked him why; and then he said, "Thou shalt know", and took him by the arm to have had him to the counter. Then all the young men resisted the aldermen, and took him from Master Munday, and cried "Prentices and clubs!" Then out at every door came clubs and weapons, and the alderman fled, and was in great danger.'

The rising became general. The mobs broke open the prisons and released those who had been jailed for offences against aliens. The mayor and sheriffs caused a proclamation to be read in the King's name, but were not obeyed, but as the mobs came to St. Martin's Gate they met Sir Thomas More who made a speech to them entreating them to go home 'and had almost brought them to a stay' when stones thrown hit a sergeant-at-arms, and at once all was brawl again. In that co-operative literary effort of Elizabethan times, the play *Sir Thomas More*, the scene of More's speech to the crowd (which bears Shakespeare's signature in every line) is the best of a badly constructed drama. Thomas More is made to appeal, first, to the leaders of the riot to command silence among their followers, and Lincoln, a riot leader, replies, 'A plague on them, they will not hold their peace; the devil cannot rule them.' That answer provides More with the opening for a majestic oration:

MORE: Then what a rough and riotous charge have you,
To lead those that the devil cannot rule?—
Good masters, hear me speak.

DOLL: Aye, by the mass, will we, More: thart a good
housekeeper and I thank thy good worship for my
brother Arthur Watchins.

ALL: Peace, peace.

MORE: Look, what you do offend you cry upon,
That is the peace, not [noise] of you heare present:
Had there such fellows lived when you were babes,
That could have topt the peace, as now you would,
The peace wherein you have till now grown up
Had been ta'en from you, and the bloody times
Could not have brought you to the state of men.
Alas, poor things, what is it you have got,
Although we grant you get the thing you seek?

BETT: Marry, the removing of the strangers, which cannot
choose but much advantage the poor handicrafts of
the city.

MORE: Grant them removed, and grant that this your noise
Hath chid down all the majesty of England;
Imagine that you see the wretched strangers,
Their babies at their backs and their poor luggage
Plodding to the ports and coasts for transportation,
And that you sit as kings in your desires,
Authority quite silenced by your brawl,
And you in ruff of your opinions clothed;
What had you got? I'll tell you: you had taught
How insolence and strong hand should prevail,
How order should be quelled; and by this pattern
Not one of you should live an aged man,
For other ruffians, as their fancies wrought,
With self-same hand, self reasons, and self right,
Would shark on you, and men like ravenous fishes
Would feed on one another . . .

After that brilliant rebuke of xenophobia and rebellion (which would to God our own age had taken to heart); More tells them that in rising against foreigners, they are in arms against the Lord. The rioters cry, 'Marry, God forbid that!' Then follows a remarkable political statement:

MORE: Nay certainly you are;
   For to the king God hath his office lent
   Of dread, of justice, power and command,
   Hath bid him rule, and will'd you to obey;
   And, to add ampler majesty to this,
   He hath not only lent the king his figure,
   His throne and sword, but given him his own name,
   Calls him a god on earth. What do you, then,
   Rising 'gainst him that God himself instals,
   But rise 'gainst God? what do you to your souls
   In doing this? O, desperate as you are,
   Wash your foul minds with tears, and those same hands,
   That you like rebels lift against the peace,
   Lift up for peace, and your unreverent knees,
   Make them your feet to kneel to be forgiven!

His speech concludes by asking them—if you are exiled for to-day's affairs, where will you go but to foreign soil? And see what you have taught foreigners to do to strangers!

The Elizabethan dramatists who concocted this play do not know what More said on that occasion, any more than we do —though there may have been a city tradition. We may accept that these doctrines were Shakespeare's, for they bear the stamp of his order-loving mind, but were they More's? The answer must be a qualified yes. All More's writings confirm his respect for authority, his Christian sense of its divine origin, his hatred of dissension. His record in office underlines what he wrote in *Utopia*, or *The Apology*, or *Dialogue of Comfort*. Why then—I think we must ask—his early epigrams against tyrants, his feel-

F          81

ing for equality, his own rejection of the King's authority? The answer is that More's respect for the office did not blind him to the deficiencies of whatever man might hold it. The kingly office was the opposite of a tyranny: it was an office hedged round by obligations. The King was bound under oath to preserve the law, and under the most solemn contract imaginable swore allegiance first to God. Rebellion was unthinkable against a king, but the King's powers were not unlimited and he could not usurp in man's soul that allegiance which every man, like the King himself, owed to God. Yet, all the same, we can be sure that More would not have been quite so ready as Shakespeare to identify God and the King.

When the riots had been put down and the streets silenced by patrols of armed men, many prisoners were taken, some boys of thirteen years of age. Thirteen were found guilty of high treason and gallows were set up all over the city. But when the principal rioter, Lincoln, had been hanged, there came an order from the King to stay the executions. A mass confession and repentance followed. On the 22nd May the King came to Westminster Hall in state, and commanded the prisoners to be brought before him. Hall records that 'Then came in the poore yonglings and old false knaves, bounded in ropes, all along, one after another, in their shirts, and every one a halter about his neck, to the number of four hundred men and eleven women. And, when all were come before the king's presence, the Cardinal sore laid to the Mayor and the commonalty their negligence, and to the prisoners he declared that they had deserved death for their offence. Then all the prisoners together cried, "Mercy, gracious Lord, mercy!" Then the lords altogether besought his grace of mercy; at whose request the king pardoned them all.'

This well-calculated display of the King's clemency was, no doubt, designed to prevent a breach between the King and the city upon which he so much depended. What share precisely More had in contriving it we do not know, but the play *Sir*

*Thomas More* attributes the King's clemency to More's intercession. The fame it brought him is evident in what the Lord Mayor said in the play, and London still obviously believed a century after the riots—

> *My lord, you set a gloss on London's fame*
> *And make it happy ever by your name.*
> *Needs must we say, when we remember More,*
> *'Twas he that drove rebellion from our door.*

In the year following Evil May Day, More became a member of the Privy Council. One other factor in securing him this honour was his handling of a court case in which he was counsel for the Pope against the King. A ship of the Pope's had arrived at Southampton, and the King held it in forfeit. More was briefed by the papal ambassador to fight the papal case and did so with such skill that, according to Roper, 'both was the said forfeiture to the Pope restored, and himself among all the hearers, for his upright and commendable demeanour therein, so greatly renowned, that for no entreaty would the King from henceforth be induced any longer to forbear his services'.

Manifestly, More was a growing power in the land. His authority in London, for so young a man (he was not yet forty) was surely unique. He was one of the greatest of the group of humanists whose cause Henry VIII and Cardinal Wolsey had both espoused. He was the author already of *Utopia*, *Richard the Third*, *Life of Pico della Mirandola*, a lawyer and a judge of distinction. He was the spokesman of the intellectuals, of the reforming party within the Church, and of the City of London. Moreover, as *Utopia* was designed to show, he was a man with a political programme. The fact that he was *not* a king's man, and had earned the opprobrium of Henry VII in a matter in which every merchant in England was on the boy's side, not the King's, made him the greater prize for Henry VIII, if he could be captured. The young King did more than seek to capture him, he sought to captivate him, and he succeeded in drawing one of the strongest and most independent minds in the kingdom into his service. From now on the relations between Henry and Thomas More dominate our story.

CHAPTER FIVE

# THE SINGULAR FAVOUR
# OF PRINCES

The rising young lawyer, Under-Sheriff of London, first entered the King's service in 1515 as ambassador to Flanders in company with Dr. Cuthbert Tunstall, and Dr. Richard Sampson. Wolsey's choice of More was a shrewd one, but it may have been involuntary, for Roper says that it was 'at the suit and instance of the English merchants, he [More] was, by the King's consent, twice made Ambassador in certain great causes between them and the merchants of the Stilliard'. The Steelyard, in the city, was the headquarters of the Hansa merchants who settled there in 1250. More embarked upon this troublesome trade embassy armed not only with the authority of the King, but with letters of introduction from Erasmus to the town clerk of Antwerp, the learned Peter Giles, and the friendly talks of the two men during negotiations which dragged out for six months are immortalized in the opening epistle of *Utopia*, addressed to Giles.

In this, More excuses himself for delay in sending to Giles his book on the Utopian Commonwealth, for his other cares and troubles, he pleads, have left him little time for writing. 'Whiles, I do daily bestow my time about law matters: some to plead, some to hear, some as an arbitrator with mine award to determine, some as an umpire or a judge, with my sentence to discuss. Whiles, I go one way and visit my friend: another way about mine own private affairs. Whiles, I spend almost all day abroad among others, and the residue at home among mine own; I leave to myself, I mean to my book, no time. For when I am come home, I must commune with my wife, chat with my children, and talk with my servants. All the which things I reckon and account among business, forasmuch as they must of necessity be done: and done they must needs be, unless man will be stranger in his own house. . . . Among these things now rehearsed, stealeth away the day, the month, the year. When do I write then? And all this while I have spoken no word of sleep, neither yet of meat, which among a great number doth waste no less time than doth sleep, wherein almost half the lifetime of man creepeth away. I therefore do win and get only that time, which I steal from sleep and meat.'

Upon this busy and conscientious man the shadow of the King's demands had fallen. He knew what was going to be asked of him eventually, and in the First Book of *Utopia* the merits and dangers of the King's service are closely argued. It is to Raphael Hythloday, after he has recited some of his travels and experiences, that Peter Giles makes a remark which opens up the personal preoccupations of More: 'Surely Master Raphael I wonder greatly, why you get not into some king's court. For I am sure there is no prince living, that would not be very glad of you, as a man not only able highly to delight him with your profound learning, and this your knowledge of countries, and peoples, but also meet to instruct him with examples, and help him with counsel. And thus doing, you shall bring yourself in very good case, and also be of ability to help all your friends and kinsfolk.'

Raphael replies that he has done enough for *them* already and does not see why, for their sakes, he should give himself in bondage to kings, to which Giles protests that bondage was not in his mind, but rather his friend's advancement to a wealthier condition. What, replies Hythloday, to a wealthier condition when my mind is clean against it? 'Now I live at liberty after my own mind and pleasure, which I think very few of these great states and peers of the realms can say.' At this point More puts himself into the discussion with the significant plea of public duty—'you shall do as it becometh you: yea, and according to this wisdom, to this high and free courage of yours, if you can find in your heart so to appoint and dispose yourself, that you may apply your wit and diligence to the profit of the weal public, though it be somewhat to your own pain and hindrance. And this you shall never so well do, nor with so great profit perform, as if you be of some great prince's council, and put into his head (as I doubt not but you will) honest opinions and virtuous persuasions.'

The discussion continues. Hythloday warns More that 'the most part of all princes have more delight in war-like matters and feats of chivalry (the knowledge whereof I neither have nor desire) than in the good feats of peace: and employ much more study, how by right or wrong to enlarge their dominions than how well and peaceably to rule and govern that they have already.' And has he, he asks, sufficiently taken into account the corruption of flattery and jealousy? At this point the discussion about the merits of the king's service breaks off and there follows the long social and political criticism of England which will be considered in another chapter. At the end of it, the discussion is resumed, and More says, once again in the first person, with the air of a man who has looked at this problem from all sides; 'But yet, all this notwithstanding, I can by no means change my mind, but that I must needs believe, that you, if you be disposed, and can find in your heart to follow some prince's court, shall with your good counsels greatly help and further the commonwealth. Wherefore there is nothing more appertaining to your duty, that is to say, to the duty of a good man. For whereas your Plato judgeth that weal publics shall by this means attain perfect felicity, either if philosophers be kings, or else if kings give themselves to the study of philosophy, how far I pray you, shall commonwealths then be from this felicity, if philosophers will vouchsafe to instruct kings with their good counsel?'

There follows a shrewd (but disguised) discussion of the foreign policy of Henry and Wolsey, whose incessant war-like scheming was thoroughly distasteful to More. Now supposing, Hythloday asks, if I, in the midst of this, sought to tell the King to be content with his own kingdom, and not to meddle with other kingdoms, 'how think you it would be heard and taken'? ' "So God help me, not very thankfully," ' More replies. On home affairs, the traveller asks—suppose I were openly to tell the prince how to run his government so that he shall be feared of evil men and loved of good 'how deaf hearers think you should I have?' "Deaf hearers doubtless," replies More, who soon after makes a judicial summary of the problem. It is, in brief, that the best is the enemy of the good. 'If evil opinions and naughty persuasions cannot utterly and quite be plucked out of their [the rulers'] hearts, if you cannot, even as you would, remedy vices, which use and custom hath confirmed: yet for this cause you must not leave and forsake the commonwealth: you must not forsake the ship in a tempest, because you cannot rule and keep down the winds. . . . For it is not possible for all things to be well, unless all men were good.'

Between 1515 and 1516, therefore, Thomas More made the decision that he ought not to refuse to enter the King's service, upon the moral grounds that unless good men are prepared to advise the King, bad men will. The year 1516, in which More announced this decision in *Utopia*, was a hopeful one, for everywhere the prestige and influence of the humanists was rising. In that year appeared the *New Testament* of Erasmus, with its call to a purer Christian life. In that year, too, he published his *Institute of the Christian Prince*, dedicated to the young Charles of Spain who had just come to the throne. It is a book such as might have been written for Christian rulers (were any to be found) after the First World War. Now was the moment when the new men might enter the councils of the young princes of Europe and guide them towards the ideal of good government at home, and peace and unity in Europe.

HENRY VIII
After Holbein, artist unknown

# THE SINGULAR FAVOUR OF PRINCES

If we are to understand the More of 1516 it is important not
to let his end cast a shadow over his prime. *We* know to what
his decision led; to him, in 1516, the future was mercifully hidden. Henry VIII, at his accession, a warm-hearted boy of nineteen, was the princely embodiment of the hopes of the humanists. His ultimate moral degeneration and tyranny were no
more to be imagined by his contemporaries than More's
martyrdom, or Luther's triumph. Thomas More spoke of him,
in his poem in which he celebrated the accession, as combining
all the attributes of a man, with a feminine beauty, like Achilles
in woman's guise. Another eye-witness wrote: 'His Majesty is
the handsomest potentate I ever set eyes on; above the usual
height, with an extremely fine calf to his leg; his complexion
fair and bright, with auburn hair combed straight and short in
the French fashion, and a round face so very beautiful that it
would become a pretty woman, his throat being rather long
and thick. . . . He speaks French, English, Latin, and a little
Italian; plays well on the lute and harpsichord, sings from the
book at sight, draws the bow with greater strength than any
man in England, and jousts marvellously.' And Mountjoy
burst into raptures, in writing of him to Erasmus: 'When you
know what a hero he now shows himself, how wisely he be-
haves, what a lover he is of goodness, what affection he bears to
the learned, I will venture to swear that you will need no wings
to make you fly to behold this new and auspicious star. Oh, my
Erasmus, if you could see how all the world here is rejoicing in
the possession of so great a Prince, how his life is all their desire,
you could not contain your tears for joy. The heavens laugh,
the earth exults, all things are full of milk, of honey, and of
nectar. Avarice is expelled the country. Liberality scatters
wealth with a bounteous hand. Our King does not desire gold
or gems or precious metals, but virtue, glory, immortality.'

And it turned out happily to be true that during the first
fifteen years of his reign one of Henry's great passions was the
new learning in which he aspired to shine himself by the book

he wrote in defence of the Pope against Luther, *Assertion of the Seven Sacraments*. Erasmus spoke of his court as an example to the world in learning and piety, and praised the manner in which he sought to promote learning among the clergy. There were more men of learning in the English court than at a university, according to one statement. As a Prince he had corresponded with Erasmus; as a King he took the side of the reforming 'Greeks' against the hidebound 'Trojans' at the universities. Was he not either the philosopher-prince, or the prince surrounded by philosophers, of whom the humanists dreamed? Historians have noted the clemency and toleration of the early years of his reign. When Colet, in 1513, that war-fevered year, preached before the King and his Court exhorting men to follow the example of Christ rather than Caesar, voices were raised against him, and the King himself feared for the effect such talk would have upon the morale of the expedition ready to move against France. He sent for him and talked with him, and finally dismissed him in the most friendly way before those who had abused him, saying, 'Let every man have his own doctor, this is mine,' and drinking his health.

For More to have hesitated, in 1515 or 1516, before the King's offer of friendship might even have been the cause of damage to the things most dear to More's heart. And it was friendship, not simply advancement, which the young King offered. We are apt to think of Erasmus as More's greatest friend, and the King as his enemy. Yet for years More saw far more of the King, and of the King as friend, than ever he saw of Erasmus. From 1518, when More became Master of Requests, until 1532, when he resigned from the Chancellorship, More was as much in the King's company as any man's. Their company delighted each other, and the King was flattered to have a man of such wit and learning at his court. Roper speaks of the King's 'singular' favour. And such it seems to have been. Many times 'used the King upon holidays, when he had done his devotions to send for him [More] into his private room, and there some time in matters of Astronomy, Geometry, Divinity, and such other faculties, and some time in his worldly affairs, to sit and confer with him, and other whiles would he in the night have him come up to the leads, there to consider with him the diversities, courses, motions, and operations of the stars and planets. And because he was of a pleasant disposition' and, we may add, also because he was an admirer of Queen Katherine, 'it pleased the King and Queen, after the Council had supped, at the time of their supper for their pleasure commonly to call for him, and to be merry with them. When he perceived so much in his talk to delight, that he could not once in a month get leave to go home to his wife and children (whose company he most desired) and to be absent from the Court two days together, but that he should be sent thither for again, he much misliking this restraint of liberty, began thereupon somewhat to dissemble his nature, and so by little and little from his former mirth to disuse himself, that he was of them from thenceforth no more so ordinarily sent for.' More once wrote to Erasmus that he would not strain at a little fib where it was necessary, but this dissembling of his candid nature must nevertheless have been difficult. Certainly the King's friendship was not abated by it. If we are to search for evidence of their intimacy we need look no farther than the answers More made to his accusers at the time of his examination by the King's commissioners over the matter of the Holy Maid of Kent. Then he spoke of conferences with the King over his book and over the divorce in such a manner as to suggest that he had long been high in the King's confidence. And at his evident distress at his inability to help the King with the divorce since he believed it to be unlawful, and had advised the King so, the King's answer, that he would not molest him on a matter against his conscience, was still the answer of a friend to a friend, rather than of a King to his servant.

Roper, whose own ingenuous character shines so innocently through the pages of his memoir of his father-in-law, recorded with delight the evidence of the King's singular favour. 'And for the pleasure he took in his [More's] company, would his grace suddenly come home to his house at Chelsea to be merry with him, whither on a time unlooked for he came to dinner, and after dinner in a fair garden of his walked with him by the space of an hour holding his arm about his neck. As soon as his Grace was gone, I rejoicing, told Sir Thomas More, how happy he was, whom the King had so familiarly entertained, as I had never seen him do to any before, except Cardinal Wolsey, whom I saw his Grace once walk with arm in arm. "I thank our Lord, son," quoth he, "I find his Grace my very good lord indeed, and I do believe he doth as singularly favour me as any subject within this Realm. Howbeit (son Roper) I may tell thee, I have no cause to be proud thereof. For if my head would win him a castle in France (for then there were wars between us) it should not fail to go." '

If we are to take that story as it stands, then the friendship was all on one side; the King it was who wooed, and More was content to be wooed for the service he might do the commonwealth, or because he could do no other. Yet the bitterness in the reply reveals More's preoccupations with his relationship to the King. If the King were as other men, then a friendship was possible which would make its own conditions, and no one would be hurt by the ending of it. But the King was not as other men. His estate set him apart. His friendship was a condescension, his wrath was death. He was subject to pressures other men were free from, and could give rein to passions other men dared not indulge. When More retired from the Chancellorship he gave this advice to his successor, 'Mr. Cromwell, you are now entered into the service of a most noble, wise, and liberal prince; if you will follow my poor advice, you shall, in counsel giving unto his Grace, ever tell him what he ought to do, but never tell him what he is able to do, so shall you show yourself as a true faithful servant, and a right worthy Councillor. For if the lion knew his own strength, hard it were for any man to rule him.' More had by then spent some fourteen years pondering over the service owed to princes, and had argued it out with himself to the bitter end, as is shown by that retort of his to the Duke of Norfolk, when his life and liberty were endangered by his opposition to Henry. Said Norfolk, ' "By the mass (Mr. More) it is perilous striving with Princes, and therefore I would wish you somewhat to incline to the King's pleasure. For by God's body (Mr. More) *Indignatio principis mors est.*" "Is that all, my Lord?" (quoth he) "Then (in good faith) the difference between your Grace and me is but this, that I shall die to-day and you to-morrow." '

# CHAPTER SIX

# FIRST AND LAST THINGS

U topia—'nowhere'—was England's first great political tract. It was not, of course, the first political tract in *English*, for it was written in Latin, and published in Europe in that tongue prior to publication in England. There were even vernacular translations on the Continent before, in 1551, Ralph Robinson made the English translation used in this book. *Utopia* was expressly modelled upon Plato's *Republic* and like that masterpiece it sought to lay down the constitution for an ideal commonwealth, but by the happy device of purporting to describe a real community visited by 'a certain stranger, a man well stricken with age, with a black sunburned face, a long beard, and a cloak cast homely about his shoulders, whom by his favour and apparel forthwith I judged to be a mariner' with whom More talked in Antwerp. So many wonders were breaking upon Europe just then through the tales brought back by voyagers to the Indies and the Americas, that nothing seemed beyond belief, not even Utopia. And as More tells us in his dedicatory epistle 'there be with us certain men, and especially one virtuous and godly man, and a professor of divinity, who is exceeding desirous to go unto Utopia: not for a vain and curious desire to see news, but to the intent he may further and increase our religion, which is there already luckily begun.' And since Utopia was published there have been endless men and movements striving to reach it, not by land or sea, as the Vicar of Croydon would have travelled, but by means of reform or revolution. *Utopia* gave a word to the languages of the world and was mother to a brood of literary offspring—Bacon's *New Atlantis*, Harrington's *Oceana*, Bellamy's *Looking Backward*, Morris's *News from Nowhere*, Samuel Butler's *Erewhon*, and the innumerable Utopias of H. G. Wells, *A Modern Utopia*, *The Dream*, *Food of the Gods*, and even T. S. Eliot's *Idea of a Christian Society* may be put in this class. The Utopian longing is the dream of the perfected worldly society which inspired Robert Owen's 'New Harmony', the co-operative commonwealth of the Rochdale Pioneers, the absolutely free man of anarchism, and the classless society of Karl Marx. Its influence upon the political ideas of Europe is beyond computation, and with some justice political philosophers count Thomas More as the father of modern socialism. Karl Kautsky, in that Marxist classic, *Thomas More and his Utopia*, so esteems More as the rationalist and socialist of his own stamp that he is compelled to dismiss the Christian More as beyond comprehension. More's *theological* treatises, he wrote, 'became less serene and sometimes bore an ecstatic and fanatical character,' as he grew older . . . 'he said in them things which contradicted his former principles, as expressed, for instance, in *Utopia*. An investigation as to how such a change came about belongs rather to the realm of psychology than of history. For us they have merely a pathological interest. . . .'[1] That was a view once widely held.

*Utopia* is divided into two books. It is the second which describes the Utopia visited by Raphael Hythloday, and the first which embarks upon a criticism of sixteenth century society. More's personal problem about entry into the King's service, about which he writes in the First Book, has already been discussed, and it remains therefore to summarize More's political and social criticism. The traveller Hythloday claimed to have visited Cardinal Morton and to have taken part in a long discussion about England's social conditions which arose from his forthright assertion that 'the punishment of thieves passeth the limits of justice, and is also very hurtful to the weal public. . . . For simple theft is not so great an offence, that it ought to be punished with death.' So flat a contradiction of the view of the three estates of the realm needed careful justification, and Hythloday proceeded to present a case for the *social* responsibility for crime—'what other thing do you, than make thieves and then punish them?'

The view that man is what his environment makes him is to be found crudely and violently argued in the writings of another great Utopianist, Robert Owen, and is perhaps inseparable from any attempt to draw up the conditions for an ideal commonwealth. Nevertheless what More put forward was not clogged by dogma; it was the practical vision of a lawyer and statesman, that one must not drive people to dangerous measures by oppressive and unjust institutions, customs and laws. For how is it, he asked, that despite all our savage punishments, we still have so many thieves among us? Would it not be better to provide the unlucky with 'some means whereby they might get their living, so that no man should be driven to this extreme necessity, first to steal, and then to die'?

Where do we recruit our thieves? From ex-soldiers, to begin with, who maimed or lamed, or old and past teaching, have no resort but to beg or steal. Then, there are too many gentlemen who, to live in idleness, exploit their tenants and drive them to beggary. Many such gentlemen keep 'at their tails a great flock or train of idle and loitering serving men' who never learn a trade or craft and know no other way of living than 'with a sword and a buckler . . . to strut through the streets with a bragging look'. Their pampered lives disincline them for honest labour—but when the master dies and they are thrust out of doors, what becomes of them? There is a far worse evil—that sheep are thrusting men out of their homes. The moving and oft-quoted passage reads: 'forsooth my lord (quoth I) your sheep that were wont to be so meek and tame, and so small eaters, now, as I hear say, be become so great devourers and so wild, that they eat up, and swallow down the very men themselves. They consume, destroy, and devour whole fields, houses and cities. For look in what parts of the realm doth grow the finest and therefore dearest wool, there noblemen and gentlemen, yea and certain abbots, holy men no doubt, not contenting themselves with the yearly revenues and profits, that were wont to grow to their forefathers and predecessors of their lands, nor being content that they live in rest and pleasure nothing profiting, yea much annoying the weal public, leave no ground for tillage, they inclose all into pastures; they throw down houses; they pluck down towns, and leave nothing standing, but only the church to be made a sheep-house. . . . Therefore that one covetous and insatiable cormorant may compass about and inclose many thousand acres of ground within one pale or hedge, the husbandmen be thrust out of their own, or else by cunning or fraud, or by violent oppression they be put besides it, or by wrongs and injuries they be so wearied, that they be compelled to sell all: by one means therefore or by other, either by hook or by crook they must needs depart away, poor, silly, wretched souls, men, women, husbands, wives, fatherless children, widows, woeful mothers, with their young babes, and their household. . . .'

More's compassion is as high as his denunciation is strong. Enclosures were a burning grievance of the England of Henry and of Wolsey, and neither was unaware of it, as it happens, for there was an act passed in the year that More was writing *Utopia* against the 'Pulling down of Towns' (7 Hen. VIII) and More's exposure of the evil may have resulted in the Commissions of Inquiry Touching Inclosures set up all over the country in 1517, which led presumably to the Acts of 1533. It is significant, too, that the agrarian programme of the Pilgrimage of Grace, the abortive Catholic rebellion of 1536, demanded the surrender of all enclosures made since the days of Henry VII.

More went on to attack the commercial spirit which was destroying the medieval rural economy, the buying cheap and selling dear, and its other aspect, the endeavours of the rich men

'to buy up all, to engross and forestall, and with their mono-
poly to keep the market alone as please them'. The curtain is
lifted on the medieval metropolitan world of 'bawds, queans,
whores, harlots, strumpets, brothel-houses, stews, and yet another stews, wine-taverns, ale houses and tippling houses, with
so many naughty, lewd and unlawful games, as dice, cards,
tables, tennis, bowls, quoits', all of which, he believes, take
money from men and force them to steal when it is gone. In
the same puritan temper he pleads for the restoration of hus-
bandry and tillage, the renewal of cloth-working and the training of men in trades and crafts. This is the way to get rid of the
social problem. Let us look to all this, he demands, and not be
so ready to put it down by vindictive punishments. As Christians it is appalling to think that we are, in defiance of the com-
mandments of God, 'so hasty to kill a man for taking a little
money'. Yet his own remedy is harsh enough, for he would
have thieves put in bondage; a condition, in fact, of slavery, not
simply imprisonment. To summarize, in his social criticism
More reveals himself as a conservative, defending the relatively
stable medieval social order against the new commercial and
materialist spirit which was undermining it.

After this bold examination of the home policy of his
country, More turned to foreign policy. But here the ground
was so dangerous that he cast his criticism of Henry and Wolsey in the form of a discussion of *French* foreign policy. The
French, he said, 'beat their brains and search the very bottom
of their wits' as to how to keep Milan, conquer the Venetians,
attach Naples to the French King's side, or to extend his do-
minion over the Low Countries. The debate of his council is
all as to the best means of doing this; whether to make temporary alliances which can be treacherously broken when expedi-
ent, or to bribe this prince or that, or buy up Swiss or German
mercenaries. And all the time his counsellors are fearful as to
what England will do next, and whether they can best fend
her off by supporting the Scots. More's advice to his own King,

through this disguise, is that he should not meddle with France, or papal temporal affairs, 'but to tarry still at home'. By a parable he tells His Majesty to give up his foolish claim to the throne of France. The Achorien King, he relates, advanced a claim to the crown of another country in order to conquer it. But when he had done so he found himself involved in so many troubles—uprisings, lawlessness and so forth—and the cost was so great to his own kingdom that at last his subjects got together and gave him free choice, either to rule one country or the other, but not both. More is blunt: 'forasmuch as no man would be content to take him for his muleteer, that keepeth another man's mules besides his.' It was a warning which supported the doctrine advanced later, that there was a social contract, from which the King derived his authority. 'The commonalty chooseth their King for their own sake and not for his sake; to the intent, that through his labour and study they might all live wealthily safe from wrongs and injuries: and that therefore the King ought to take more care for the wealth of his people, than for his own wealth, even as the office and duty of a shepherd is in that he is a shepherd, to feed his sheep rather than himself.' And this pronouncement is made at the end of an argument that the King is bound by the law, and must not seek means to evade it, or to twist it to his private ends.

The first book ends with an unequivocal argument for common ownership. 'Where possessions be private, where money beareth all the stroke, it is hard and almost impossible that there the weal public may be justly governed, and prosperously flourish.' No social justice is possible while private property is tolerated. 'No equal and just distribution of things can be made, nor that perfect wealth shall ever be among men, unless this propriety be exiled and banished. But so long as it shall continue, so long shall remain among the most and best part of men the heavy and inevitable burden of wretchedness.'

The Second Book is, to one reader at least, somewhat tedious. The static and well-ordered lives of the Utopians have a flattening effect upon me, so that when I read that it is the custom of the Utopians to attend early morning lectures, my reaction is —what on earth does anyone find to lecture about? Nevertheless, if Utopia as a home fails to charm one, the provisions More deemed necessary for good and wise government are of absorbing interest. There are three classes, or groups, in Utopian society. The bondmen, who are criminals or slaves bought from the gallows of other lands, the husbandmen and handicraftsmen (in which class all seem to be trained), and above them an 'order of the learned' to which the studious craftsmen can be promoted. From this order of the learned, which resembles more the clerisy of T. S. Eliot's *Idea of a Christian Society* than Plato's ruling class, the rulers and their officers are chosen. Government is hierarchical, for every thirty families or farms choose a 'philarch' or headman, and the headmen come together and elect a chief philarch, and these, to the number of 200, assemble to elect a prince. 'The prince's office continueth all his lifetime, unless he be deposed or put down for suspicion of tyranny.' It is rather like the election of a Pope by the College of Cardinals. The secrecy of the government is maintained, for it is an offence, punishable by death, to discuss the affairs of government outside the proper councils.

The inhabitants of Utopia, save that they are married and bring up children, live rather like monks in a monastery or students at a well-disciplined university. Their days are strictly regulated from the early morning lectures, to the hour of play after supper, and even their games are moral lessons. Hours of work are limited to six per day, and this is made possible because in Utopia there are no idle people, in the whole state, in fact, no more than five hundred people who for age, sickness or special licence are discharged from labour. The austerity extends to clothes. Like monks, they are dressed alike, wearing one coarse woollen cloak of natural colour. Of course, they scorn jewels, precious metals, and all fine personal decorations as baubles for children, and laugh at the diplomats who come arrayed in them.

Marriage is a very rational affair. The bride is displayed naked to the bridegroom before marriage, so that the bridegroom shall have nothing subsequently to regret, and the number of children per household is kept in check by moving surplus children from the large families to the small ones. Pre-marital adultery is sharply punished, but divorce by mutual consent and with the authority of the Council is permitted, and adultery is regarded also as a ground for divorce. Even suicide is allowed to a man who finds his life a torment. The Utopians have little liberty of movement. No man is allowed out of his own precincts without the authority of his prince. If he does move without his internal passport he is brought back as a runaway, and for a second offence becomes a bondman. On the other hand, once furnished with the authority of the prince he is provided with transport and everywhere freely entertained.

The houses of Utopia are distributed by lot, and periodically redistributed, and a housewife may draw freely from the common market what she needs for the well-being of her family. But 'it were a folly to take the pain to dress a bad dinner at home, when they may be welcome to good and fine fare so nigh hand at hall.' There most eat, while the elder children 'stand by with marvellous silence'. When it comes to war, the Utopians prefer to hire the soldiers of other lands to do their fighting for them, 'for they had rather put strangers in jeopardy than their own countrymen: knowing that for money enough, their enemies themselves many times may be bought and sold, or else through treason be set together by the ears among themselves.' No doubt More's experiences of European diplomacy had given birth to this cynicism.

Until the arrival of Raphael Hythloday, the Utopians had no knowledge of Christianity. There were different forms of religion in various parts of the island, but they tolerated each other. All, however, agreed 'that there is one chief and principal God, the maker and ruler of the whole world'. There was liberty to believe what a man chose, with the important exception 'that no man should conceive so base and vile an opinion of the dignity of man's nature, as to think that the souls do die and perish with the body; or that the world runneth at all adventures governed by no divine providence.' If a man chose not to believe this, they put him to no punishment, but 'count [him] not in the number of men'. He is virtually outlawed or excommunicated, for a man who has no faith in God cannot be trusted to honour the commonwealth. In pointed contrast then to tolerance over the *form* of religion is the rigid upholding of its essential content.

More speaks of an effort to introduce Christianity to Utopia which ended in disaster, and reveals his mind in what is a pointed criticism of the fanatical puritanism already abroad in Europe in 1515. A certain baptized Utopian, 'began against our wills, with more earnest affection than wisdom, to reason of Christ's religion; and began to wax so hot in his matter, that he did not only prefer our religion . . . but also did utterly despise and condemn all other, calling them profane, and the followers of them wicked and devilish and the children of everlasting damnation.' The Utopians banished him 'not as a despiser of religion, but as a seditious person and a raiser up of dissension among the people'. As to priests, they were of 'exceeding holiness' and therefore very few. Women were not excluded from the priesthood. All priests were chosen of the people, but after being chosen were quite immune from the temporal power. In dim-lighted churches the Utopians burnt incense and lighted tapers, for by these things they felt themselves lifted up, 'not supposing this gear to be anything available to the divine nature, as neither the prayers of men'. Such ceremonies were pleasant and did no harm. But no image of God was shown anywhere.

When Hythloday finally contrasts the order and beauty of the Utopian life with what was going on elsewhere, he comes to the conclusion that in all these other commonwealths (or, in other words, in Christian Europe) 'which nowadays anywhere do flourish, so God help me, I can perceive nothing but a certain conspiracy of rich men procuring their own commodities under the name and title of the commonwealth'—an interesting anticipation of Marxist theory.

Professor R. W. Chambers, in his authoritative *Thomas More*, disposed of the argument current so long, and so flattering to the English reformation, that More was teaching a protestant creed. 'What is remarkable, then, about the religion of Utopia is not the extent to which it differs from the practice of the medieval church, but the extent to which it coincides with it,' he remarks. The communion of saints, the resurrection of the dead, the life everlasting, are all within it. The tolerant religion of the Utopians contains without dispute those things the Protestants most hated. And those who are most despised in Utopia are precisely the reformers who, in the name of religious liberty, raise up sedition and dissension everywhere. There are differences nevertheless between the Utopian religion and Christianity. They are of a sacramental kind. The Utopians had come to their creeds by reason or natural theology. They were without the blessing of the revelation. Since they were not tied by sacraments of baptism and marriage, it was possible for them to permit suicide or divorce, or the display of a young woman naked to the man who wanted to marry her, as though she were a colt he was buying. But More does not necessarily argue that these things are permitted to Christians. It is the *general* lesson he seeks to apply, which Professor Chambers admirably summarized: 'With nothing save Reason to guide them, the Utopians do this; and yet we Christian Englishmen, we Christian Europeans . . . !'

Yet though the Kautsky point of view, that More was a rationalist and a communist, and his religious side merely pathological, is easily disposed of, to the ruin of so many enlightened and protestant accounts of More, his doctrine of felicity is less easy to reconcile with his other writings. *Utopia* anticipates political doctrines which were to be especially the distinction of such philosophers as Hobbes, Locke, Hume and Bentham (to say nothing of our own Bertrand Russell). One was the doctrine of the social contract, and another was that of felicity. Of the first, I have already spoken, and as to the second More says that the 'chief and principal question' which the Utopians debate is in what 'the felicity of man consisteth'. And after having weighed the matter very diligently they think 'that all our actions, and in them the virtues themselves, be referred at last to pleasure, as their end and felicity. Pleasure they call every motion and state of the body or mind wherein man hath naturally delectation. Appetite they join to nature, and that without a good cause. For like as, not only the sense, but also right reason coveteth whatsoever is naturally pleasant. . . .' That sounds indeed like the first attempt to define the pleasure-pain principle of morality which has since bloomed perennially in English philosophy. And the Utopians admit that if moral safeguards were withdrawn or 'disanulled' 'then without any delay' every man would 'do all his diligence and endeavour to obtain pleasure by right or wrong, only avoiding this inconvenience, that the less pleasure should not be a let or hindrance to the bigger: or that he laboured not for that pleasure which would bring after it displeasure, grief or sorrow.'

How then are moral safeguards maintained? Here More, the catholic theologian, is in evidence. The Utopians 'join unto the reasons of philosophy certain principles taken out of religion' because without them it is not possible to arrive at a true notion of felicity. The principles are these, that the soul is immortal, and ordained by God to felicity, and 'to our virtues and good deeds rewards be appointed after this life, and to our evil deeds punishments'. Thus a man's felicity is *not* just his earthly pleasure, *but his immortal state*. If he does evil in this world to gain pleasure, he risks enjoying the smaller 'felicity' at the expense of the greater. Hence it is by eternal felicity that we are to measure our earthly life. So, within a religious framework (but only within it), the Utopian doctrine of felicity is shown to be a reasonable one.

A man, More argues, is not under compulsion to go through this life full of misery and grief—no matter how religious he may be. In a paragraph which reveals one source of More's merriness and friendliness we read: 'For a joyful life, that is to say a pleasant life is either evil, and if it be so, then thou should-est not only help no man thereto, but rather, as much as in thee lieth, withdraw all men from it, as noisome and hurtful, or else if thou not only mayst, but also of duty art bound to procure it to others, why not chiefly to thyself? To whom thou art bound to show as much favour and gentleness as to other. For when nature biddeth thee to be good and gentle to other she commandeth thee not to be cruel and ungentle to thyself.' This is indeed a felicitous doctrine. But the doctrine of felicity carries the obvious danger, of which we should take note, that even under the aspect of eternity, good is performed for the reward of pleasure, and not for its intrinsic value. For were evil to bring the reward of eternal felicity, then it would be 'good' to do evil. Thomas More certainly believed no such thing; indeed he himself includes a warning about 'felicity' in *Utopia*. The Utopians, he says, are almost too much inclined to defence of pleasure, and to the argument that man's chief happiness resides in it. Of course, *Utopia* is more than a jest or satire on England; it is what the centuries have accepted it to be, a serious contribution to political philosophy. But when we encounter such warnings in it we should be chary of accepting the theories expressed as necessarily More's own. Indeed, his exposition of the doctrine of felicity may very well be intended as a friendly criticism of the views of Valla and Erasmus. Laurentius Valla, the Italian scholar who denounced the Donation of Constantine, was an extreme hedonist much admired by Erasmus: he took a pagan view of sensual pleasure.[2]

If we want to see the religious More in the round, we must have recourse to his other works, to *The Four Last Things*,

*Dialogue of Comfort,* and *Treatise on the Passion* in particular.
There is a remarkable change of mood between *Utopia* and
*The Four Last Things* written six to seven years later (1522).
*Utopia* sparkles and exhilarates with the hopes and fervours of
the humanists. *The Four Last Things* rejects 'such as make this
world their heaven and their lust their God'. It has the bluntness of the murals depicting the Dance of Death in old St.
Paul's. Thomas More has moved from Plato's *Republic* to *The
Confessions of St. Augustine.* The argument of felicity is left behind and it is now 'the abandonment and refusing of carnal
pleasure and the ensuing of labour, travail, penance and bodily
pain' which bring forth the Christian man. The cause of this
profound change of mood is not to be looked for in any personal failure. Sir Thomas More was a rising man, knighted the
year before, destined for the highest office, and with the confidence of the King and the country behind him. He was where
he had decided both in his poem on 'Fortune' and in *Utopia* it
was a good place to be, the holder of such an office (he was
then sub-treasurer and member of the King's council) as enabled him to give wise advice to the King and good service to
the commonwealth.

The cause may be looked for in the rise of the Lutheran
heresy, the feebleness of the papacy, and the religious dissensions which were causing Sir Thomas such sorrow, or in the
wars of European princes and their indifference to the con-
quests of the Turks. Yet we must search deeper. More continued to grow spiritually all his life. He never ceased to grow
towards God, and no writings show this better than his last,
written in the Tower, some in charcoal, under the shadow of
death. He was forty-four when he wrote *The Four Last Things,*
and the forties are notoriously a climacteric for man, and it was
as though, in writing this work (which he never succeeded in
finishing), he had at last weighed up the vanity of earthly
things, and come to see the iron necessity for the soul to orient
itself towards eternity.

## FIRST AND LAST THINGS

What grand prose it is! Here is the birth of the English language in all its vigour and beauty in an essay which, full of the religious intensity of a Savonarola, has the force and rhythm of William Langland, the fire of Shakespeare, the bluntness of Donne. When we are sick, More says, the physician sends a bill to the apothecary and on it is written a costly receipt for our cure. But listen to what is said in the scriptures and you shall find a wholesome recipe for the greatest of all sicknesses. 'Remember thy last things, and thou shalt never sin in this world.' Here, says More, 'is a short medicine containing only four herbs, common and well known, that is to wit, death, doom, pain, and joy'. Meditate on them, and you must surely see that even our hunger and sleep are a form of sickness, 'and thus mayest thou surely see that all our whole life is but a sickness never curable, but as an incurable canker, with continual swaddling and plastering botched up to live as long as we may, and in conclusion undoubtedly to die of the same sickness, and though there never came other. So that if you consider this well, thou mayest look upon death, not as a stranger, but as a nigh neighbour. For as the flame is next the smoke, so is death next an incurable sickness; and such is all our life.'[3] We die continually as we live.

There is no remedy for death. 'but as condemned folk and remediless in this prison of the earth, we drive forth awhile some bound to a post; some wandering abroad; some in dungeon; some in the upper ward; some building them bowers and making palaces in prison; some weeping; some laughing; some labouring; some playing; some singing; some chiding; some fighting; no man, almost remembering in what case he standeth, till that suddenly, nothing less looking for, young, old, poor and rich, merry and sad, prince, page, Pope, poor soul priest, now one, now other, sometimes a great rabble at once, without order, without respect of age or estate, all stripped stark naked and shifted out in a sheet, be put to death in divers wise in some corner of the same prison, and even there thrown in an hole, and either worms eat him under ground, or crows above.'⁴ The conviction that earth is a prison was one which haunted Sir Thomas. It is expressed again, with even more force, in *Dialogue of Comfort* written in the Tower, where More asks why he should grieve to find himself in prison; in what sense is the lot of a man cast into a jail any different from that of an ordinary person, whose whole life is prison?

Are you a young man? he asks in *The Four Last Things*. Count not on that. Our Lord has made no contract with us about the length of our lives. 'Reckon how many as young as thou have been slain in the selfsame ways in which thou ridest, how many have been drowned in the selfsame waters in which thou rowest.'

If this is the truth of the human situation, that we are all under condemnation, what folly lies in gluttony, lechery and covetousness. 'As for the glutton, [he] is ready to hear of temperance, yea and preach of fasting himself, when his belly is well filled,—the lecherous, after his foul pleasure past, may suffer to hear of continence, and abhorreth almost the other by himself. But the covetous man, because he never ceaseth to dote upon his goods, and is ever alike greedy thereupon, whoso giveth him advice to be liberal seemeth to preach to a glutton for fasting when his belly is empty and gapeth for meat, or to a lusty lecher when his leman is lately light in his lap . . . look if ye see not some wretch that scant can creep for age, his head hanging in his bosom, and his body crooked, walk pit-pat upon a pair of pattens with his staff in the one hand and the *pater noster* in the other hand, the one foot almost in the grave already, and yet never the more haste to part with anything, nor to restore that he hath evil gotten, but as greedy to get a groat by the beguiling of his neighbour as if he had of certainty seven score years to live.'⁵

'The wickedness of the Eye' is described in wrathful prose and with a realism almost painful. We need not doubt that the wrath is turned towards himself who, in his full-blooded youth,

rejected the monastery for the world. 'And surely so falleth it
daily, that the eye is not only the cook and the tapster, to bring
the ravenous appetite of delicate meat and drink into the belly
(so far forth that men commonly say it were better fill his
belly than his eye, and many men mind it not at all till they see
the meat on the board), but the eye is also the bawd to bring
the heart to the desire of the foul beastly pleasure beneath the
belly. For when the eye immoderately delighteth in long looking of the beauteous face, with the white neck and round paps,
and so far forth as it findeth no let, the devil helpeth the heart to
frame and form in the fantasy, by foul imaginations, all that
ever the clothes cover. And that in such excellent fashion, as the
mind is more kindled in the feigned figure of his own device
than if it should haply be if the eye saw the body belly naked
such as it is indeed. And therefore saith the holy prophet,
"Turn away thine eyes from the beholding of vanities".'

His grief over the fanaticism of Lutherans is unconcealed; oh,
'the perilous pride of them that for their few spotted virtues,
not without mixture of other mortal vices, take themselves for
quick saints on earth, proudly judging the lives of their even
Christians, disdaining other men's virtues, envying other men's
praise, bearing implacable anger where they perceive themselves not accepted and set by after the worthiness of their own
estimation. Which kind of spiritual pride, and thereupon following envy and wrath, is so much the more pestilent in that
it carrieth with it a blindness almost incurable, save God's great
mercy.'

The biographer would be dishonest who did not testify to
the significance of *The Four Last Things*. No shadow has fallen
on Thomas More, but God is preparing him for his great test-
ing.

# CHAPTER SEVEN

# THE THAMES-SIDE UTOPIA

In 1523, when Thomas More had become Speaker in Parliament, he moved to Chelsea, to a house built there by him and set in gardens which stretched down to the river's edge not far from the north end of the present Battersea bridge; and it was by boat he would travel to Westminster or the city. Then Chelsea was a small village. The well-to-do had set their mansions along the water's edge. Across the river wild-fowl swarmed in Battersea marshes, and beyond them the wooded hills of the Sydenham ridge stood up against the sky. It was a rural setting by the swan-haunted reaches of a silvery river such as we cannot to-day find until we get beyond Maidenhead; the atmosphere of it was recaptured by William Morris in the opening pages of *News from Nowhere*.

In this setting, far from the stews of the city, More expanded his tiny kingdom, seeking among his near and dear ones to live that life he had set down for mankind in *Utopia*. Roper paints a picture of a pious household. 'As Sir Thomas More's custom was daily, if he were at home, besides his private prayers with his children, to say seven psalms, litany and suffrages following, [it] was his guise nightly, before he went to bed, with his wife, children, and household to go to his chapel, and there upon his knees ordinarily to say certain psalms and collects with them: and because he was desirous for godly purposes some time to be solitary, and sequester himself from worldly company; a good distance from his mansion builded he a place, called the new building, wherein was a chapel, a library, and a gallery, in which as his use was upon other days to occupy himself in prayer and study together, so on the Fridays there usually continued he from morning unto evening, spending his time duly in devout prayers, and spiritual exercises; and to provoke his wife and children to the desire of heavenly things, he would sometimes use these words unto them. "It is now no mastery for you children to go to heaven. For everybody giveth you good counsel, everybody giveth you good example. You see virtue rewarded, and vice punished, so that you are carried up to heaven by the chins. But if you live in the time, that no man will give you good counsel, nor no man will give you good example, when you shall see virtue punished, and vice rewarded, if you will then stand fast, and firmly stick to God upon pain of life, if you be but half good, God will allow you for whole good." '

There is a passage in the *Dialogue of Comfort* in which More justifies his solitary devotions. If a man wishes to think deeply of the spiritual disciplines God demands of him, then, he advises, let him do more than go to confession frequently. 'Let him also choose himself some secret solitary place in his own house, as far from noise and company as he conveniently can, and thither let him some time secretly resort alone, imagining himself as one going out of the world even straight unto giving up his reckoning unto God of his sinful living.' And we know of those other austerities with which he disciplined himself by Roper's account of them; an account which lifts the curtain once again upon a merry, and by no means intimidated family circle: 'And albeit he appeared honourable outwardly, and like one of his calling, yet inwardly he no such vanities esteeming, secretly next his body wore a shirt of hair, which my sister More, a young gentlewoman, in the summer, as he sat at supper singly in his doublet and hose, wearing thereupon a plain shirt without ruff or collar, chancing to espy, began to laugh at it. My wife not ignorant of his manner, perceiving the same privily told him of it, and he being sorry that she saw it, presently amended it. He used also sometimes to punish his body with whips, the cords knotted, which was known only to my wife his eldest daughter, whom for her secrecy above all he specially trusted, causing her, as need required, to wash the same shirt of hair.' And Dame Alice wondered where his washing went to!

The disciplines alone would tell us—if we need to be told—that it would be foolish to seek in More the rationalist or socialist of the modern sort, or even one who in his own life sought to live the Utopian doctrine of felicity. More was a medievally religious man, living every day under the sense of eternal judgment. Yet humour and good sense restrained him; austerities made public easily become an occasion for spiritual pride, and it may be against himself that he tells (in *The Dialogue of Comfort*) the parable of the man who wanted to kill himself for Jesus Christ's sake one Good Friday because Christ had died for him. He was persuaded by his wife not to take his own life, for after all, Christ had not done so, but had been killed by others. Instead she herself offered to crucify him, reminding him however that Christ had first been scourged and crowned with thorns. And so with his assent she bound him to a post and beat him; but when she brought the crown of thorns to him and would have thrust it on his head, he said he thought that was about enough for one year, but that he hoped to do the remnant the next.

Austerities cast no shadow over the More household, and across the centuries the happiness of the family reaches us. The household was large. When More moved to Chelsea, Margaret was eighteen, and already married to William Roper in 1521, her sixteenth year. Elizabeth was seventeen, and Cecilia, sixteen—a household indeed of 'jeunes filles en fleur'. Son John was fourteen. Elizabeth married Sir John Dauncey and Cecily married Giles Heron, a ward of Sir Thomas. By the most fateful coincidence, such as no novelist would dare to contrive, Giles Heron was foreman of the jury which tried Anne Boleyn; and he himself was, in his turn, martyred in 1540. John More

CECILY HERON AND MARGARET ROPER
Detail from copy by Locky at Nostell Priory of Holbein's
family group

married Anne Cresacre, and from their grandson, Cresacre
More, we have one of the many family biographies. Margaret
Gigs was an orphan adopted by More. She was the sweet child
who confessed in later life that she would sometimes commit
some trifling fault in order to bring upon herself the loving re-
proof of Sir Thomas. She married a young scholar from St.
Paul's School, John Clement, the tutor of More's children,
who became Professor of Greek at Oxford, and was another
of this staunch family to suffer for his faith. There were other
members from time to time, Harris, and Gunnell, both tutors
and secretaries, and a lady's maid, Dorothy Colley, of such distinction of person that she married John Harris, which was
equivalent to marrying into the family. When More rose in
office he was of necessity compelled to enlarge his household
with the servitors proper to his estate. But these, too, seem to
have been subject to the Utopian discipline. They were not
allowed to flirt with the serving-maids, and idleness was
frowned upon; there were to be no braggarts swaggering up
and down Chelsea with nothing better to do, and so small
allotments were given to each of them to cultivate. When
More's resignation compelled him to dismiss them, he found
posts for them all.

Stapleton tells of More going about the back lanes of Chelsea
and inquiring about poor families and relieving their distress, not
by a few groats, but according to the scale of their necessities.
This was an office which often fell to little Margaret Gigs when
More was absent, as was so often the case, on official duties. A
letter from Thomas More to Dame Alice reveals his good
neighbourliness. It was written in September 1529, when he
was Chancellor of the Duchy of Lancaster. He was with the
King at Woodstock when news came to him that, through the
negligence of a neighbour, part of his house and all his barns
full of corn were burnt down and that the flames had spread
and done damage to the property of others. Let us, he writes to
his wife, grudge not the loss, but take it cheerfully as God's

H                                      113

will, but 'I pray you to make some good enserche what my poore neighbours have lost and bid them take no thought therefore, for and I should not leave myself a spoon there shall be no poore neighbour of mine bear no loss by any chance happened in my house'.[1]

More took part in the parish life, and in Chelsea old church, More's arms were to be found engraved on the capital of an archway. But in 1940 the church was almost totally destroyed by German bombs. All that survived, the south aisle, has been roofed and restored for worship. In this church, while More was still alive, he caused a tomb to be erected for himself and his first and second wives, with his obituary written by his own hand engraved on the slab which covered it. Miraculously the slab survives and stands propped against the wall in the south aisle. It was in this now ruined church that More often served at Mass, or carried the cross in processions, not ashamed to perform an office so often passed on to the verger. Roper tells the delightful story that once, when More was Chancellor of England, the Duke of Norfolk visited him and was shocked to find him wearing a surplice and singing in the choir: 'To whom after service, as they went homeward together arm in arm, the Duke said: "God's body, God's body, (my Lord Chancellor) a parish clerk, a parish clerk, you dishonour the King and his office!" "Nay," quoth Sir Thomas More, smiling upon the Duke, "your Grace may not think that the King, your master and mine, will with me for serving God his Master be offended, or thereby count his office dishonoured." '

Sir Thomas watched over the education of his children with remarkable thoroughness. Erasmus described them as brilliant: 'A year ago it occurred to More to send me a specimen of their progress in study. He bade them all write to me, each one without any help, neither the subject being suggested nor the language corrected; for when they offered their papers to their father for correction, he affected to be displeased with the bad writing, and made them copy out their letters more neatly and accurately. When they had done so, he closed the letters and sent them to me without changing a syllable. Believe me, dear Budeé [the French statesman to whom he was describing this], I never was more surprised; there was nothing whatever either silly or girlish in what was said, and the style was such that you could feel they were making daily progress. . . . In that house you will find no one idle, no one busied in feminine trifles. Titus Livius is ever in their hands. They have advanced so far that they can read such authors and understand them without a translation, unless there occur some such words as would perhaps perplex myself. His wife, who excels in good sense and experience rather than in learning, governs the little company with wonderful tact, assigning to each a task, and requiring its performance, allowing no one to be idle or to be occupied in trifles.'[2] In a long letter to a tutor of the children, William Gunnell, More expounded his educational tenets. One of them was that it was manifest good sense that learning should be made available to women. He justifies what he knows will be attacked by saying that, since the education of women is a new thing, many will gladly assail it and blame upon it any faults in women which otherwise they would have attributed to their sex. He particularly warned the children against self-conceit: 'That this plague of vainglory may be banished far from my children, I do desire that you, my dear Gunnell, and their mother and all their friends, would sing this song to them, and repeat it, and beat it into their heads, that vainglory is a thing despicable, and to be spit upon; and that there is nothing more sublime than that humble modesty so often praised by Christ; and this your prudent charity will so enforce as to teach virtue rather than reprove vice, and make them love good advice instead of hating it.'[3]

Apart from More's eldest daughter Margaret, who was to grow in spiritual stature side by side with her father, the most interesting member of the household was 'son Roper', Margaret's husband, and brilliant first biographer of More. Roper tells us that he was sixteen years resident in the house of his father-in-law. There are some difficulties in explaining this length of residence, but they need not detain us. Suffice that Roper was an intimate and an admirer of Sir Thomas More, and to his faithful memory posterity is deeply in debt.

The early biographers of More relate the story of Roper's long contest with him over Luther's doctrines; it appears that for many years of his life Roper held tenaciously to Protestant convictions. He was so much given to devout, and as one biographer puts it, immoderate exercises, that he developed a form of religious mania. Cresacre More writes that having drunk a full draught of heresy Roper came to Sir Thomas to 'get him a licence to preach what the spirit had taught him' even from St. Paul's Cross. Sir Thomas, smiling, replied: 'Is it not sufficient, son Roper, that we that are your friends should know that you are a fool, but that you would have your folly proclaimed to the world?' But Roper continued to read Luther's works, and in the city he consorted with German merchants of Lutheran persuasion and was even brought before Cardinal Wolsey on charges of heresy. This did not effect a cure; on the contrary, it appears to have moved him to lock himself up for whole days with a Lutheran Bible.

Roper was a man who did not easily bridle his tongue, and with no effort of the imagination we can understand what kind of daily debate Sir Thomas must have been compelled to suffer at his table. Eventually, so Harpsfield tells us, More's patience was exhausted and he 'privately in his garden talked with his daughter Margaret, and said: "Meg, I have borne a long time with thy husband; I have reasoned and argued with him in these points of religion, and still given to him my poor fatherly counsel, but I perceive none of all this able to call him home; and therefore, Meg, I will no longer dispute with him, but will clean give him over and get me to God and pray for him." And soon after, as Roper verily believed, through the great mercy of God, at the devout prayers of Sir Thomas More, he perceived his own ignorance, oversight, malice and folly, and turned him again to the Catholic faith, wherein (God be thanked) he hath hitherto continued.'

It is rather odd, all the same, to find recorded in Roper's *Life* a discussion with his father-in-law in which the Lutheran heresy was talked of without his own fall from grace being mentioned. As it was at the time that the King's divorce was being generally debated, we must assume, I think, that his reconversion had been completed, and he was all zeal the other way. For, with joy, he commended to Sir Thomas, 'the happy estate of the realm, that had so catholic a Prince, that no heretic durst show his face, so virtuous and learned a clergy, so grave and sound a nobility, so loving and obedient subjects, all in one faith agreeing together', and was shocked to receive an answer proper to his naïveté: 'True it is indeed (son Roper), and yet I pray God that some of us, as high as we seem to sit upon the mountains, treading heretics under our feet like ants, live not the day, that we gladly would wish to be at league and composition with them, to let them have their churches quietly to themselves; so that they would be content to let us have ours quietly to ourselves.' This roused Roper, who proceeded to show many reasons why he believed this would be an evil thing.

' "Well, well, [More answered], I pray God (son Roper) some of us live not till that day" showing me no reason why I should put any doubt therein. To whom I said, "By my troth, Sir, it is very desperately spoken," that vile term (I cry God mercy) did I give him, who by these words perceiving me in a fume, said merrily unto me, "Well, son Roper, it shall not be so, it shall not be so". Whom in sixteen years and more, being in his house conversant with him, I could never perceive him so much as once to fume.'

More's prayers were effective on another occasion, for when Margaret Roper lay desperately ill of the sweating sickness, that evil which plagued More's age more dangerously than influenza has our own, and her recovery was despaired of: 'her father (as he that most entirely tendered her) being in no small heaviness for her . . . there in his chapel upon his knees most devoutly besought Almighty God, that it would be like his goodness, unto whom nothing was impossible, if it were his blessed will, at his mediation to vouchsafe graciously to hear his petition; where incontinent came into his mind, that a glister [enema] should be the only way to help her, which when he had told the physicians, they by-and-by confessed, that if there were any hope of health, that it was the very best help indeed, much marvelling of themselves, that they had not afore remembered it. Then it was immediately ministered unto her sleeping, which she could by no means have brought unto waking, and albeit after she was thereby thoroughly awaked, God's marks, evident undoubted token of death, plainly appeared upon her, yet she (contrary to all their expectation) was (as it was thought) by her father's fervent prayer miraculously recovered, and at length again to perfect health restored, whom if it had pleased God at that time to have taken to his mercy, her father said he would never have meddled with worldly matters after.'

Roper tells us that More's sons-in-law attempted to turn his promotion to high office to their own advantage and we recall, in this connection, that one of the arguments advanced to Raphael Hythloday to persuade him to take service under a king (and brusquely rejected) was the possibility of advancing the interests of his relations. Hythloday said he had done enough, and saw no reason to do more for them. In those days, when equalitarian procedures were not established, the most usual path to advancement was through patronage or family assistance. Is it dead even now? Certainly then there was nothing very improper to the morality of the times in the raillery to which one of his sons-in-law subjected the powerful Chancellor, saying: 'When Cardinal Wolsey was Lord Chancellor, not only divers of his privy chamber, but such also as were his door keepers got great gain, and since he had married one of

his daughters, and gave still attendance upon him, he thought
he might of reason look for somewhat.' The impudent son-in-
law went so far indeed as to suggest that More's rectitude, and
in particular his ready accessibility to all, was not very profitable to those near to him, for they could not in honesty take
gifts for what any suitor could secure on his own. More's answer is revealing in its very mildness. If he can help him by
giving priority to a case he is interested in, he is prepared to do
so, but corruption of any kind—*no!* 'If the parties will at my
hand call for justice, then were it my father stood on the one
side and the devil on the other side (his cause being good) the
devil should have right.' And when son-in-law Heron (to
whom this warning may have been addressed) in a case before
More in Chancery presumed on his relationship, More made
'a flat decree against him'.

We must not overlook the role which Dame Alice played in
Chelsea. She it was who, according even to Erasmus, not her
best friend, presided over the sunny household. We catch a
glimpse of her mocking relationship with her husband in the
story in the *Dialogue* of the good wife who 'when her husband
had no list to grow greatly upward in the world, for neither
would labour for office of authority, and over that forsook a
right worshipful room when it was offered him, she fell in hand
with him (he told me) and all too rated him, and asked him:
what will you do that you list not to put forth your self as
other folk do? Will you sit still by the fire, and make goslings
in the ashes with a stick as children do? would God I were a
man: and look what I would do. Why wife, quoth her husband, what would you do? What? by God go forward with
the best. For as my mother was wont to say, God have mercy
on her soul, it is ever more better to rule than to be ruled. And
therefore by God I would not warrant you be so foolish to be
ruled, where I might rule. By my troth wife quoth her husband in this I dare say you say truth. For I never found you
willing to be ruled yet.'[4]

And once again More's own shrewd estimate of the worth of worldly advancement follows a paragraph or two later when he says, in what must have been the same flippant discussion with Dame Alice, that 'twenty men standing bareheaded before him, keep not his head half so warm as to keep on his own cap'. And that he never got so much pleasure out of being bareheaded as he once got misery out of a cold caught through standing too long bareheaded before the King.

Is not the story in the *Dialogue of Comfort*, of the mistress who had all the words, also a story of More and Alice? 'There was of late a kinswoman . . . [whose] husband had much pleasure in the manner and behaviour of another honest man'—the merchant Bonvisi, who was so great a comfort to More in the Tower, at a guess!—'and kept him therefore much company, by reason whereof, he was at his meal time the more oft from home. So happed it on a time, that his wife and he together, dined or supped with that neighbour of theirs, and then she made a merry quarrel to him, for making her husband so good cheer out a door, that she could not have him at home. Forsooth mistress, quoth he (as he was a dry merry man) in my company nothing keepeth him but one, serve you him with the same, and he will never be from you. What gay thing that be, quoth our cousin then? Forsooth mistress quoth he, your husband loveth well to talk, and when he sitteth with me, I let him have all the words. All the words, quoth she? marry that am I content, he shall have all the words with good will, as he hath ever had. But I speak them all myself, and give them all to him, and for ought that I care for them, so shall he have them still: but otherwise to say that he shall have them all, you shall keep him still, rather than he get the half.'[5]

After More's resignation from the Chancellorship, this little jest occurred, only possible between people on affectionate and tolerant terms: 'And whereas upon the holidays, during the High Chancellorship, one of his gentlemen, when service at the church was down, ordinarily used to come to my Lady, his wife's pew, and say, "Madam, my Lord is gone," the next holiday after the surrender of his office, and departure of his gentlemen he came unto my Lady, his wife's pew, himself, and making a low courtesy, said unto her, "Madam, my Lord is gone."'

Fittingly, Roper couples this with a paragraph on how at this time More would talk with his wife and children of the joys of heaven, and the lives of the holy martyrs, who suffered imprisonment and death rather than offend God. He was reminding them of what he had warned them more than once, that they must not look to be lifted up to heaven in feather beds.

CHAPTER EIGHT

# 'THE HIGHEST ROOM IN
# THE REALM'

Wolsey, the last and greatest of the ecclesiastical statesmen of England, first appeared at court as a brilliant and able young cleric, chaplain to Henry VII. Henry VIII made him his almoner, and by 1511 he was a member of the Privy Council, moreover holding the balance between the peace party led by Archbishop Warham and the war party led by the Earl of Surrey. It was a role which he enjoyed and which he exploited to secure the King's ear and favour, and England's greatness. His ascendancy over the young King was a remarkable one, and the Venetian ambassador of those years, Sebastian Giustiniani, has recorded that when he first knew Wolsey he would say, 'His Majesty will do so and so,' but that by and by this became the first person plural, '*We* shall do so and so,' until finally the King's role was ignored and Wolsey would remark, '*I* shall do so and so'. Giustiniani was even forced to advise his government that in a certain diplomatic matter it would be advisable to present the proposal not to the King, but the Cardinal first, lest he should resent the precedence accorded to the King.

This proud and avaricious prelate had honours, sees, and pensions heaped upon him. He kept a more than royal estate, not supported by the King, however, but by the revenues of ecclesiastical preferments, a practice not uncommon in those days. At the time of his greatness, when he celebrated Mass, Bishops served for him, and when he sat at table, Dukes of the realm waited upon him as though he were the equal of Kings and Emperors. Meeting the Emperor Charles at Bruges he remained mounted on his mule and simply doffed his cap. He was in much of his behaviour more royal than the King, and his arrogance and pretensions were greatly resented by his countrymen. He became the most hated man in England, and the country rejoiced at his fall.

He was summed up by H. A. L. Fisher, in his *History of Europe*, as one who embodied 'in his own person almost every abuse which may be charged against the Catholic Church in the sixteenth century' and, Fisher goes on, 'Power, not reform, was the master passion in the breast of this son of the grazier of Ipswich, who combined in his own person the functions of Lord Chancellor, Archbishop of York, Bishop in succession of Bath and Wells, Durham and Winchester, Abbot of St. Albans, *Legatus a Latere*, and, in addition, farmed three bishoprics for non-resident aliens. But that such a man should have initiated reform was an omen of future changes.'[1]

Yet for all that neither his domestic reforms nor his foreign policy were to be despised. In the Church he dissolved some of the less efficient small monasteries and applied their endowments to the foundation of colleges; in agricultural matters he initiated a policy to block enclosures; in foreign policy he aimed to make England arbiter of Christendom. His foreign policy was a European one, but it was directed to secure his own elevation to the papacy and Henry's to the Emperor's crown. During the first ten years of Henry's reign, when he was autocrat of England, he raised the prestige of England to a height it had never before attained. The island which had fallen behind in Europe during the Wars of the Roses, and which had followed a policy of cautious isolation during the reign of Henry VII, now blossomed out as a power able to challenge France and Spain.

It was the delusion of grandeur, however, made possible by the treasure accumulated by Henry VII, and by the even bal-

ance of the two great contenders for European domination,
France and Spain. But the treasure of Henry VII was not inex-
haustible, as Henry and Wolsey discovered, and England's
striking power on the Continent was severely limited by the
fact that she could not keep an army in the field for much
longer than three months. England could raid, and harry, but
she could not occupy, and it was spoil as much as victories her
army sought. When, in 1523, Thomas More wrote a long
letter concerning military policy to Wolsey, at the King's com-
mand, we find in it a paragraph which witnesses to the difficulty experienced in keeping an army in the field without the
promise of loot:

'Finally where the Duke adviseth that the King's army shall
in marching [through France] proclaim liberty, sparing the
country from burning and spoil, the King's Highness thinketh
that sith his army shall march in hard weather with many sore
and grievous incommodities, if they should also forbear the
profit of the spoil, the bare hope whereof, though they get
little, was great encouraging to them, they shall have evil will
to march forward and their captains shall have much ado to
keep them from crying Home! Home!'[2]

At the opening of Henry's reign, his Queen, Katherine of
Aragon, widow of his deceased elder brother Arthur, was un-
official ambassador for her father, Ferdinand of Spain. The
atmosphere was a honeymoon one. France was the natural
enemy, Spain the natural ally, particularly in view of English
trade with the Low Countries. All went well until the campaign of 1512, in which Henry, in a generous gesture of loyalty
to his father-in-law, sent an expedition to attack the French in
the Bay of Biscay. Ferdinand failed to make junction with the
expedition. He left it high, and save for his lachrymose pro-
testations, dry, and it was allowed to wilt there all through the
summer. In vain the soldiers looked for aid from Spain. The
men died of dysentery, the discipline suffered, indignation
against Spain ran higher, and finally the army brought itself

home. If it was not mutiny, it was the next thing to it. It is significant that soon after this the propriety of Henry's marriage was first mooted, only to be dropped when the diplomatic weathercock swung Spainwards again.

Even such an inexperienced king as Henry then was, could see that the desertion and humiliation of England must have been calculated. He had been made a pawn in another monarch's game, and a far less courageous king would have felt bound to redeem his honour. Henry's retaliation was not to break with Spain but to launch his own brilliant campaign in France the following year, into which Wolsey, the architect of the manœuvre, threw himself with tremendous zest. In March the greatest navy England had ever seen left to harry and blockade the French ports. In June the King embarked to join his army assembling at Calais. He rode among the troops, athletic, glowing, regal. Victory followed victory until finally Tournay, the richest city in northern France, fell in September and Henry was able to return home with the honours thick upon him, and the valour of English arms demonstrated to a surprised continent. It was a warning to the wily Ferdinand that England was no longer negligible.

Wolsey's skilful diplomatic game enabled him to engineer the general truce of 1518 which so much rejoiced More, Erasmus and the humanists. There came out of all this that fateful and intoxicating year, 1520, when both Francis I, and Charles V (who had secured election to the German emperorship which Henry coveted), courted the alliance of England. Francis and Henry met in all the ostentation of chivalry at the Field of Cloth of Gold. They and their queens demonstrated their official amity in gilded pavilions, with trains of velvet and satin-clad courtiers rustling around them, and the armour of the jousts clashing in their honour. They made believe that by exchanges of valour they could seal their friendship and hold the peace of Europe as though the Round Table had never passed away.

## 'THE HIGHEST ROOM IN THE REALM'

Charles the Emperor sought England's friendship rather more subtly in the almost surreptitious visit he paid to Kent. England was making promises to both sides, but like a coy virgin was determined not to yield herself to either bidder if it could be helped. But could it be helped? When war came in 1522 England had to decide which side to join, a painful dilemma when in any fight she was bound to be the loser if her ally was the victor. Henry was bankrupt, and the real interest of England was to avoid a clash at all, and by an uncommitted neutrality. But the prizes of war were too great a temptation, and no doubt Charles dangled them effectively enough—the papacy for Wolsey, and the restoration of the crown of France to Henry. Here Wolsey made his most serious mistake in foreign policy, in the decision to support Charles. He miscalculated the aid which England could give, overestimated the French, underestimated the Emperor. The result was that Francis suffered a crushing defeat at Pavia in February 1525, when his royal person was taken prisoner.

The war to save, among other things, the papacy from French influence, ended by handing over virtually the whole Continent to the power of Charles. England's own role had been so contemptible that she could exercise no restraining influence on her powerful ally. The discredited papacy, the creature of the Emperor, was servile and impotent, and in 1527, partly as a result of the mistakes of English policy, Rome was sacked. Among the imperial troops were thousands of Lutheran *landsknechts*, toughs who were as much to be feared as the Turks themselves, and who believed themselves the scourge of God against the Babylonian whore. They marched on Rome and with other soldiery forced an entry, and raped, looted and burnt across the city. The Pope, Clement VII, fled to the castle of St. Angelo. The horses of the soldiery were stabled in St. Peter's, before the high altar, and the most sacred places desecrated. The corrupt and cynical Rome of the Renaissance Popes was left in ruins. This dread event, which left so deep an impression on the mind of Thomas More, seemed to signal the end of Christendom itself, for what the Lutherans were doing in the north, the Turks were doing in the south, and in 1529 the Turkish Army camped outside Vienna, firing its cannon over her walls, and the marks of the cannon-balls may still be seen upon her towers. Wolsey's humiliation was complete when the peace of Cambrai in 1529 virtually ignored England. When he fell, medieval ecclesiasticism came crashing with him. The Church in England had no powerful protector left. England, once again, was a third-rate power, and another fourteen years were to pass before she crossed swords again with France.

Sir Thomas More served under Wolsey. Much use was made of his eloquence and negotiating skill. He was in Flanders on a commercial embassy when the scheme for *Utopia* was born. He was present at the Field of Cloth of Gold, was engaged upon the negotiations with the Emperor at Bruges and Calais, on the embassy to Amiens in 1527, and at Cambrai in 1529. In fact, he had a hand in all the important foreign negotiations between 1520 and the time of his appointment to the Chancellorship, and was so often abroad on them or dancing attendance on the King that one wonders how often really he saw his home and children.

More had declared his attitude to Wolsey's foreign policy in the pages of *Utopia*; we have already seen that it involved the strongest strictures on policies of aggression and aggrandisement pursued at the expense of the body of Christendom. In his official letters to his chief, More is extremely cautious, and refrains from any expressions of opinion. We may be certain however that his anti-war sentiments were well known to the King and the Lord Chancellor. It was the suspicion that More was not sorry to see the war taxes cut down by Parliament in 1523 which led to Wolsey's indignation at More's conduct as Speaker. In that year of intoxication, when Henry was expecting Bourbon, Constable of France, to overthrow Francis, and the French to welcome Henry as their king with glad cries of

# 'THE HIGHEST ROOM IN THE REALM'

'Vive le roi d'Angleterre!' More injected a quiet note of realism into the prevailing hysteria with his comment to Wolsey: 'I pray God if it be good for his grace and for this realm, that then it may prove so, and else in the stead thereof, I pray God send his grace an honourable and profitable peace.'

More's deep concern, indeed dismay, over Wolsey's European policy arose from his consciousness of its ultimate futility. He saw more clearly than most statesmen of the times that the day had arrived when, come what might, France was going to be governed by a monarch of her own choice, Germany by a German, Spain by a Spaniard, and that, dynastic accidents apart, nations were not going to submit to be ruled by monarchs who did not incarnate the new national will. The risks and chances of war undertaken to break the national spirit of other countries were too great. One stroke of bad fortune could throw everything in peril, despite the pouring out of treasure and of life. Even where campaigns were brought to success, the difficulty of governing another country was almost insurmountable; it drained energies which ought to be available for the pressing problems left at home. More's policy was, if you will, an isolationist one, but with this difference—More felt the reality of Christendom in his bones; and the wars of princes across it were as grievous to him as a civil war in his own country. If he wanted England to isolate herself from the quarrels of princes, it was because he hoped that thereby she might give better service to the whole of Christendom which was threatened both by internal dissension and external enemies. Nothing shows up his mood in those years better than the *Dialogue of Comfort* which is cast in the form of a discussion with a Hungarian nobleman whose country faces destruction by the Turks. Sometimes the chief Turk of whom More is thinking is Henry VIII. At other times 'the Turks' are clearly the Lutherans. Quite often they are the real Turks. 'Hungary', he writes in one paragraph, 'hath been ever hitherto a very sure key of Christendom. And out of doubt if Hungary be lost, and

128

that the Turk have it once fast in his possession, he shall ere it be long after, have an open ready way into almost the remnant of all Christendom, though he win it not all in a week, the great part will be won after I fear me, within a very few years.' Nevertheless, 'if we people of the Christian nations, were such as would god we were, I would little fear all the preparations that the great Turk could make.'

Thomas More was a statesman of Christendom where Wolsey was little more than an adventurer. Roper tells us that 'on a time walking along the Thames side with me at Chelsea, in talking of other things, he said to me, "Now would to God, son Roper, upon conditions three things were well established in Christendom, I were put in a sack, and here presently cast into the Thames." "What great things to be these, Sir," quoth I, "that should move you so to wish?" "Wouldest thou know, son Roper, what they be?" quoth he. "Yea, marry Sir, with a good will if it please you," quoth I. "I'faith, they be these, son," quoth he. "The first is, that whereas the most part of Christian princes be at mortal wars, they were at universal peace. The second, that where the Church of Christ is at this present sore afflicted with many heresies and errors, it were well settled in an uniformity of religion. The third, that where the King's matter of his marriage is now come into question, it were to the glory of God and quietness of all parties brought to a good conclusion:" whereby, as I could gather, he judged, that otherwise it would be a disturbance to a great part of Christendom.'

In the *Dialogue*, these propositions are made again, in almost the same terms, save that the matter of the divorce is not mentioned, for Henry had by that time taken the law into his own hands. The conclusion in the *Dialogue* is a summons to Christians to rally 'in defence of Christendom against our common enemy the Turk'. More expressly addresses this appeal to the German heretics.

More did not like the new monarchy. He made the sove-

reign in Utopia removable on suspicion of any designs to en-
slave the people. He cast contempt on such notions as that the
King can do no wrong, and is above the law. He therefore
detested Wolsey's high-handed methods of exacting money
for the King's pocket without parliamentary sanction, or twist-
ing ancient laws to the King's advantage. This is specifically
denounced in *Utopia*. Why then did More serve under Wolsey? We must understand that, then, there was no party system,
and no rigid divisions or well-marked political lines such as all
democratic countries are familiar with to-day. The King
governed; policy emanated from him to his ministers. The
ministers advised. More was serving the King, not Wolsey, and
it was perfectly possible for More to hold views opposed to
those of Wolsey, yet continue to serve. Such a matter was for
the King to decide. And certainly More's discretion was so
considerable that he would never have gone out of his way to
announce his opinions to Wolsey or the King. It is necessary to
say this in order that More's one open clash with Wolsey can
be understood.

Sir Thomas More was chosen Speaker to that Parliament
hastily assembled by Wolsey in 1523 to vote Henry money to
continue his war against France. Henry and Wolsey had for-
merly commanded sufficient treasure to govern without Parlia-
ments, and even now when the need was evident Wolsey was
chary of calling them because of the anti-clerical and anti-
despotic feeling to which they instinctively gave voice. Without doubt More was considered a good choice both by Henry
and Wolsey, not only for his forensic skill, but because he was
one of the King's men, privy to his policy, and to be relied
upon (it was thought) to keep Parliament on the King's side.
Upon being chosen More first 'disabled' himself for his unfit-
ness for the honour and asked for his discharge and, as Edward
Hall the chronicler relates, in a witty manner:

'One Phormio desired Hannibal to come to his reading,
which thereto assented, and when Hannibal was come he be-

gan to read, *de re militari*, that is of Chivalrie, when Hannibal perceived him, he called him an arrogant fool, because he would presume to teach him which was master of Chivalrie, in the feats of war. So the speaker [More] said, if he should speak before the king of learning and ordering of a common wealth and such other like the king being so well learned and of such prudence and experience might say to him as Hannibal said to Phormio. Wherefore he desired his grace that the commons might choose another speaker: The Cardinal answered, that the king knew his wit, learning and discretion by long experience in his service: wherefore he thought that the commons had chosen him as most metest of all, and so he did admit of him.'

Sir Thomas More then presented two important petitions to the King; Roper devotes several pages of his brief memoir to them, for they were petitions establishing both the immunity and privilege of the Speaker, and freedom of speech in the Commons. Hall's summary tells us that More asked, 'if he should be sent from the commons to the king on message and mistake their intent, that he might with the king's pleasure resort again to the commons for the knowledge of their true meaning: The other was, if in communciation and reasoning any man in the common house should speak more largely than of duty he ought to do, that all such offences should be pardoned, and that to be entered of record.' The two petitions were granted, and Parliament opened its debate.

Wolsey complained of the Parliament that no sooner was anything said in it than it was blown abroad in the alehouses. This complaint did not please the burgesses. Wolsey, feeling it necessary to come before Parliament himself to explain the necessity for the subsidy the King was demanding, informed Parliament of his pleasure. Then Sir Thomas More, notwithstanding that he was the King's servant, proved himself a real Parliament man, for he advised Commons not to receive the Cardinal with a few of his lords, but with his whole train, 'with all his pomp, with his maces, his pillars, his pollaxes, his crosses, his hat, and great seal too', so that if it should turn out that he had occasion to grumble again about leakages from Parliament, 'we may be the bolder from ourselves to lay the blame upon those that his Grace bringeth with him'.

Wolsey appeared in all his state, and explained, according to Hall, 'how the French king, Francis the first, called the most Christened king, had so often times broken his promise with the king of England and his wellbeloved nephew Charles the Emperor, that the king in his honour could not longer suffer'. Not only had he failed to observe the articles of the tripartite Treaty between England, France and the Emperor, and withheld tributes and other payments, 'but also he hath sent John duke of Albany into Scotland, to make war and to invade this realm'. For this reason the King had determined on war, and war cost money, and Parliament was there to raise it. What Wolsey demanded was the fifth part of every man's goods, 'that is to say four shillings of every pound, for he said that the year following the King and Emperor should make such war in France as hath not been seen'.

Wolsey made the mistake of insisting on an answer from the Commons there and then. But the Commons remained silent, not stomaching either the tax or the manner in which their consent to it was demanded. Wolsey pressed them, as Roper records, thus: 'Masters, ye have many wise and learned men among you, and seeing I am from the King's own person sent hither unto you for the preservation of yourselves and all the Realm, I think it meet you give me a reasonable answer.'

He met with no response and so began to hector individual members of the chamber to compel them to declare themselves. No one was prepared to break the rule of the Commons, that they answered only through their Speaker. 'Masters, unless it be the manner of your house (as of likelihood it is) in such causes to utter your minds by the mouth of your speaker, whom ye have chosen for trusty and wise, (as indeed he is) here is without doubt a marvellous obstinate silence.' The Cardinal thereupon required the answer of More, who excused himself reverently upon his knees, saying that he could not know what to answer for the house until they had first discussed the matter among themselves and instructed him. Wolsey had no recourse but to retire.

Commons rejected Wolsey's demand on the ground that it would be ruinous to the country, that there was not the coin available to pay such a tax and that it could only bring hardship on those who would have to sell land in order to pay the tax and afterwards resort to barter in order to eat. When Wolsey was approached to persuade the King to take a smaller sum, he answered in a rage that he would rather have his tongue plucked out by pinchers than do so. He came down to the House again, in the role of the devil rebuking sin, to persuade the Commons that the luxury of the land alone showed that the tax demanded was a feasible one. However, the Commons offered only a graduated tax beginning at no more than two shillings in the pound, which made the Cardinal very wroth. 'Whereupon the Cardinal displeased with Sir Thomas More, that had not in this Parliament in all things satisfied his desire, suddenly arose and departed; and after the Parliament ended, uttered unto him all his griefs, saying, "Would to God you had been at Rome, Mr. More, when I made you Speaker". "Your Grace not offended, so would I too, my Lord," ' More replied, and thereupon broke off discussion of Parliament and began to talk of the Cardinal's gallery at Hampton Court and other pleasant subjects. The Cardinal waited a more convenient opportunity to show his displeasure. Presently it was proposed to send More as ambassador to Spain, but More refused, protesting in a rage that it would be sending him to his grave, where he could ill serve His Majesty. To which Roper tells us that the King replied, 'It is not our meaning, Mr. More, to do you hurt, but to do you good we would be glad. We therefore for this purpose will devise upon some other, and employ your service otherwise.'

Since More, as Speaker, had strictly maintained parliamentary privileges and decisions even against the King's first minister, whereas he might have played the role, for which he was obviously chosen, of persuading Parliament to bow to the King's will, the King's intervention in the matter of the Spanish embassy was not ungenerous. He was not, in such matters as these, the man to bear a grudge. Nor, surprisingly enough, was Wolsey, for immediately after the dissolution of Parliament, Wolsey wrote to the King to ask for More the customary rewards for the Speaker, and after praising More's service said, 'I am the rather moved to put your Highness in remembrance thereof, because he [More] is not the most ready to speak and solicit his own cause'.

More's own letter to Wolsey shortly afterwards, in which he speaks mostly of the King's war, ends with a personal note which suggests that he himself was unchastened by the parliamentary affair:

'Furthermore it may like your good Grace to understand that at the contemplation of your Grace's letters, the King's Highness is graciously content that besides the £100 for my fee, for the office of the Speaker of his Parliament, to be taken at the receipt of his Exchequer, I shall have one other hundred pounds out of his coffers, by the hands of the Treasurer of his Chamber, wherefore in most humble wise I beseech your good Grace that as your gracious favour hath obtained it for me so it may like the same to write to Mr. Wyatt that he may deliver it to such as I shall send for it, whereby I and all mine, as the manifold goodness of your Grace hath all ready bound us, shall be daily more and more bounden to pray for your Grace, whom our Lord long preserve in honour and health.'[8]

In 1525 More was made Chancellor of the Duchy of Lancaster. Whatever Wolsey's feelings may have been the King had obviously decided not to throw away the services of so valuable a statesman. He may already have been looking ahead, to Wolsey's successor.

## 'THE HIGHEST ROOM IN THE REALM'

In June 1527, so Hall tells us in his *Chronicles*, Cardinal Wolsey appeared before the King and said, concerning the fateful sack of Rome, 'Sir, by the only calling of God, you be made Defender of the Christian faith: now consider in what state the Church of Christ standeth: see how the head of the Church of Rome is in captivity; see how the holy fathers be brought into thraldom, and be without comfort: now shew yourself an aid, a defender of the Church, and God shall reward you.'

To which Henry made reply: 'My Lord, I more lament this evil chance than my tongue can tell, but where you say that I am defender of the faith, I assure you, that this war between the Emperor and the Pope is not for the faith, but for temporal possessions and dominions, and now sith the Bishop Clement is taken by men of war, what should I do? my person nor my people cannot rescue him, but if my treasure may help him, take that which to you seemeth most convenient.'

The people, Hall says, were less bothered about the fate of the Pope than of their money, and were much annoyed when Wolsey gathered together a quarter of a million pounds to aid him, and set out in great pomp and splendour for the Continent as though personally to ransom the Pope. With twelve hundred horse, and as glorious a train as though he were a monarch, Wolsey passed through London on the 3rd of July and headed for the coast. He stopped, on the second night, at Rochester, where the wise Fisher was bishop. And there one purpose of this gilded journey became evident, for Wolsey sounded Fisher about the royal divorce, and swore him to secrecy. The royal divorce had become urgent, and there might be difficulties in the way of securing it from a Pope who was the prisoner of Katherine of Aragon's imperial nephew.

Wolsey and his train, and his barrels of gold so begrudged by the people, were taken on board ship and landed at Calais. From Calais the golden cavalcade set out with Cuthbert Tunstall, Bishop of London, Lord Sandys, the King's Chamberlain, the Earl of Derby, Sir Henry Guildford, Sir Thomas More and many other knights and squires jingling along in it. They rode first to Boulogne, where a pageant greeted them at the gates 'in the which was a Nun called holy church and three Spaniards and three Almayns had her violated, and a Cardinal her rescued and set her up of new again'. And people whispered that they never imagined a Cardinal had such power.

The procession of state, impressive and glorious as it was intended to be, was rather more designed for the salvation of Wolsey than of the Pope. All Wolsey's cunning was now essential if he were to avoid ruin. The victory of Charles over Europe made a violent switch of English policy necessary, but it had to be undertaken in such a way as not to endanger the required papal dispensation for the divorce. That would best be done by freeing the Pope from the Emperor, but it might also be secured by freeing the Church from the Pope. It was rumoured in Spain, which had most to fear from these conspiracies, that Wolsey had gone to France to separate the Churches of England and France from the Holy See and to have himself declared Pope of the schismatic Church. Had he succeeded in securing a sufficient number of cardinals to repudiate the papal authority while the Pope remained in the Emperor's hands, that schism would in fact have been accomplished. As it was, this part of the policy proved a damp squib. Only three French Cardinals and one Italian were found willing to repudiate Clement, and they were probably bought. True, on the 17th August a treaty of peace was concluded in the cathedral of Amiens, amid much magnificence, but this was small gain. The delegation remained to enjoy the festivities and did not reach home until the end of September.

Wolsey returned without having engineered a revolt of Christendom against the Pope, with the Pope still captive, and more alarmed than ever about the trouble Henry's desire for a divorce might bring upon him, and with a Treaty which frightened the English with the threat of war against Spain and the destruction of the Netherlands trade. In January 1528, as

Englishmen feared, the Anglo-French declaration of war against Spain was made. Public opinion was so hostile that open warfare was just not to be thought of. Negotiations were set on foot to save the Flanders trade, and in June a truce was arranged. In 1529 the Treaty of Cambrai was concluded, from which the English were in effect excluded. Henry had served both his allies badly, and deserved well of neither. Wolsey was not present at the negotiations—the English delegation consisted of More, Tunstall and Hackett, and it found itself compelled to sign conditions agreed to in advance by Charles and Francis, of which the most fatal was the surrender of Italy to the imperial sphere of influence.

## CHAPTER NINE

# THE GREAT DIVORCE

What was the character of that high and puissant prince, Henry the Eighth of England? He was of all kings of the day most the product of the Renaissance, tutored by its scholars, encouraged by its thinkers, learned in its theology, and almost idolized as the incarnation of the golden age of which Erasmus dreamed. That so much hope was pinned upon him was itself an indication of the new attitude to princes. Why should not such hopes have been made to rest upon the Church, or the universities, or the merchant classes? The fact is, it was not so; on the contrary these powerful institutions looked to Henry as their protector and friend. The moral decline of the papacy in those years was itself the consequence of the decision that it was more important even for the Pope to be a strong temporal prince than a spiritual power. Princely power, as Machiavelli's textbook for the ambitious indicated, was the proper goal of political realism. The growth of national consciousness everywhere called up in its train a new awe and fascination in the face of princely authority. A divinity began to attach itself to these privileged and pampered beings. Nothing could be done in the face of their opposition. Only they could control the tumultuous and subdue rival factions.

Henry began his reign as a generous, intelligent prince well content to be guided by those with experience in the government of the country, filial still in his thinking, and happy so long as he could pursue the sports and festivities for which he had an overriding passion. But the great advantage in the hands of the powerful prince is continuity of office. Advisers come and go, the prince remains. His accumulated experience would have made Henry difficult to resist in the end even if no magical aura of kingliness had surrounded him. Henry learnt the business of England, and learnt it well, and like many a contemporary dictator came to identify the nation he governed with himself. England was Henry's, and Henry's will and passion were England's policy. The more one studies his reign, the more difficult it becomes to separate the private ends from the public interests. He learnt what More feared he would, not only what he should do, but what he could, and not the least was that 'he would be obeyed, whosoever spoke to the contrary'. Corrupted by power, and by his sensual appetites, he came to believe in his own moral impunity. 'The elevation and isolation of his position fostered a detachment from ordinary virtues and compassion, and he was a remorseless incarnation of Machiavelli's Prince.'[1]

When his marriage with Katherine produced six dead children, including two dead princes, and only one living daughter, a sense of Nemesis completely medieval in character fell on him. His terrible dread of having offended against God's holy laws must never be underestimated in any judgment of his proceedings over the divorce. It is one part of the source of the passion with which he pursued his ends, the cost notwithstanding. What was remarkable was the manner in which he was able to subordinate this real sense of guilt to the diplomatic necessities. As far as the facts went, he was living with his brother's widow, she who as child-bride had consummated her marriage with her child-husband in Ludlow Castle, and he was now the victim of the curse on incestuous unions which no papal dispensation could remove. This, it seemed, certainly justified getting rid of Katherine when the political relations with Spain dictated at the same time the expediency of this. The two motives became impossible to distinguish in his behaviour, however carefully he might himself plead only the moral excuse for divorce. But the invalidity of the moral plea was demonstrated by the fact that he proposed to marry Anne Boleyn, whose sister had been his mistress. That which was the cause of his divorce from Katherine was held to be no barrier to his marriage to Anne. It is difficult to penetrate into such a mind.

Long before Wolsey set foot in France in 1527, with all his glorious train, moves to annul the marriage had begun. In April of that year the King sent a Dr. Richard Wolman to Winchester to discuss the matter with the redoubtable Bishop Fox. Wolsey had been instructed to discuss the matter under bond of secrecy with Bishop Fisher of Rochester. What Henry said was plain enough. He had noticed for some years past in reading the Bible the severe penalties which had been inflicted by God on those who married the relicts of their brothers, and he had come to the conclusion that the deaths of his male children by Katherine were a Divine judgment for his breach of a Divine law.

In May of the same year, Wolsey, as papal legate, summoned Henry before him to render account of his conduct in living with his brother's widow. The proceedings were formal, and intended to put the matter in order from an ecclesiastical point of view. Henry had not applied for a divorce: he had been summoned to give reasons as to why he should think he was married at all. Was it necessary at this point to secure a papal dispensation to annul the marriage? Could not Wolsey have made the necessary declaration that the marriage was invalid, and left it to the Pope to endorse? If the Pope failed to do so, such a decision might have been attributed publicly to his captivity and the whole dispute thrown to the doctors of the church. There was a lot to be said for facing the Pope just then with the accomplished fact. There were excellent contemporary precedents for exactly such a proceeding, and in England too, for the Duke of Suffolk had been divorced in this manner, and a papal bull confirming it had been forthcoming. The worldly-wise Popes had come to recognize that royal personages were pawns in the complicated dynastic snakes and ladders of Europe, and conceded to them divorce rights not accorded the common people. Henry's sister, Margaret, Queen of Scotland, had only recently been granted a divorce by papal authority, on grounds which were a scandal. By precedent, Henry's divorce should have presented no problems at all. Why then did not Wolsey act in the light of these precedents? It is difficult to know. Wolsey was playing his own game; he may genuinely have sought to give the King the absolute protection of a papal bull; he may on the contrary have prayed that a papal refusal would quash the proceedings, hoping against hope that Henry would not go to the lengths of a break with Rome; he may simply have been playing for time, anticipating that the King would grow tired of Anne, as he had already grown tired of her sister; he knew that a friendly papal solution of the matter would strengthen the hand of both Pope and Wolsey in England. Certainly his failure himself to grasp the nettle becomes more incomprehensible when we recall that time and again during the negotiations Wolsey warned the Pope that refusal to grant the divorce would ruin the Church in England, and perhaps cut her off from the Holy See. In effect the only answer from Rome was a petulant shrug; was it the Pope's fault that people became heretics?

Wolsey sought to hide the negotiations with the papacy from Emperor Charles. Attempts were made to prevent Katherine from communicating with her nephew. They proved useless. At the time that Wolsey was on his way abroad secretly to summon the cardinals to defy, if necessary, the captive Pope, the Emperor dispatched a cardinal to Rome to defend Katherine and to secure if possible the revocation of Wolsey's legatine powers.

The Pope conceded Wolsey's demand to send a legate to England to try the case of the King's divorce, but he, Cardinal

Campeggio, came with secret instructions to postpone judgment. Let us concede it, it was a perilous course for the papacy to pursue, to determine thus to humiliate a king at a legatine court in full view of his own people. It took no account of the sixteenth century temper of princes and peoples; and it emerged after all, not from moral courage but from pusillanimity. On 31st May 1529, the legatine court assembled in the hall of Black Friars, in the City of London. The King and Queen were summoned to appear before it. Katherine attended to protest that the tribunal had no power to proceed in the issue, and in a moving scene the tragically misused woman threw herself on her knees before Henry and begged for his mercy and her honour. This wrung from Henry the generous kind of gesture of which he was still capable: 'She is, my Lords, as true, as obedient, and as conformable a wife, as I could, in my fantasy wish or desire. She hath all the virtuous qualities that ought to be in a woman of her dignity, or in any other of baser estate.' But the legate would not declare his own power invalid, and Henry would not withdraw his case, and the trial went on without the Queen. Campeggio did the one thing which appeared safe to him, he procrastinated. And when on the 23rd July the King and his courtiers assembled at the court to hear the verdict, Campeggio gave none, simply adjourning the court until October on the ground that this was the vacation period in the Roman curia. 'By the mass!' cried the Duke of Suffolk, crashing his fist on the table, 'It was never merry in England since we had Cardinals among us!' Wolsey replied with spirit, but the King did not rebuke Suffolk, and from that moment Wolsey's fate was sealed. Soon after, the Great Seal was taken from him by the Dukes of Norfolk and Suffolk. He was banished to the north and visited (for the first time) his see of York, where arrangements were made for his installation, and thousands came to implore his blessing. He made the mistake of asking Francis I to intercede with Henry in his cause, and was betrayed by his Italian barber who accused him also of urging Pope Clement to excommunicate Henry. He was arrested for treason and began a journey back to London which had it been fulfilled could only have ended in the block. At Leicester Abbey an attack of dysentery forced him to rest. 'I am come', he told the monks, 'to lay my bones among you.' On his death-bed he spoke of the King to the Lieutenant of the Tower, his warder. 'He is a Prince of a most royal courage: sooner than miss any part of his will, he will endanger one half of his kingdom: and I do assure you I have often kneeled before him, sometimes for three hours together, to persuade him from his appetite, and could not prevail. And, Master Knyghton, had I but served God as diligently as I have served the King, He would not have given me over in my grey hairs. But this is my due reward for my pains and study, not regarding my service to God, but only my duty to my prince.'

Wolsey's fall, a year before his greatness came crashing down in death, made Thomas More Lord Chancellor. The Great Seal was delivered to him by the King at Greenwich on 25th October 1529. The significance of this escaped no one. The great but hated prelate was gone. About the failures of his foreign and domestic policies More had every right to be critical, for his own had been so opposed to them. But had Wolsey fallen because of these, or because he failed to secure the King his divorce, and now stood, in the minds of both King and people, for all that was hateful in clericalism? Openly the King abandoned Wolsey and gave the Seal to his known opponent, More, the layman. At one stroke the vested interest of the Church in the King's affairs was brought to an end. More's was the finest legal mind in the country, he had been as outspoken as Erasmus in his criticism of clerical corruption, was the natural man to call upon to lead Church reform, and his service to the King in the highest office, and his support for the King's divorce, if it could be secured, would be a triumph for the King. Thus must the King have calculated, and though he knew already what qualms More possessed about the divorce, he may have counted confidently on the highest office to extinguish them. Roper speaks of More's being given the office by the King 'the rather to move him to incline to his side' and describes the ceremony at Westminster Hall when the Dukes of Norfolk and Suffolk brought Sir Thomas More to his place in the Chancery and 'the duke of Norfolk, in audience of all the people there assembled, showed, that he was from the King himself straightly charged by special commission there openly, in the presence of all, to make declaration, how much all England was beholden to Sir Thomas More for his good service, and how worthy he was to have the highest room in the Realm and how dearly his Grace loved and trusted him; for which, said the Duke, he had great cause to rejoice. Whereunto Sir Thomas More, among many other his humble and wise sayings (not now in my memory) answered, That although he had good cause to rejoice of his Highness' singular favour towards him, yet nevertheless he must for his own part needs confess, that in all things by his Grace alleged he had done no more than was his duty. And further disabled himself as unmeet for the room, wherein, considering how wise and honourable a prelate had lately before taken so great a fall, he had thereof no cause to rejoice.'

The rueful and chivalrous note is typical of More.

Wolsey having failed abysmally, and the papacy having manifested its opposition, Henry turned to Parliament to execute his will. Writs for Parliament were executed in August and Parliament met soon after. Hall paints the pageantry for us: the King, he wrote, 'came by water to his palace of Bridewell, and there he and his nobles put on their robes of Parliament, and so came to the Black Friars Church where a mass of the holy ghost was solemnly sung by the kings chapel, and after the Mass, the king and all the Lords of Parliament, and Commons which were summoned to appear at that day came into the Parliament chamber, where the king sat on his Throne

or seat royal, and Sir Thomas More his Chancellor standing on
the right hand of the king behind the bar made an eloquent
oration, declaring that like as a good shepherd which not
alonely keepeth and attendeth well his sheep, but also forseeth
and provideth for all thing which either may be hurtful or
noisome to his flock, or may preserve and defend the same
against all perils that may chance to come, so the king' seeing
the abuses and enormities of the time 'had summoned his high
Parliament . . . and as you see that amongst a great flock of
sheep some be rotten and faulty which the good shepherd
sendeth from the good sheep, so the great wether which is of
late fallen as you all know, so craftily, so scabbedly, yea and so
untruly juggled with the king, that all men must needs guess
and think that he thought in himself that he had no wit to perceive his crafty doing, or else that he presumed that the king
would not see nor know his fraudulent juggling and attempts:
but he was deceived, for his grace's sight was so quick and pene-
trable that he saw him, yea and saw through him, both within
and without, so that all thing to him was open, and according
to his desert he hath had a gentle correction, which small punishment the king will not to be an example to other offenders,
but clearly declareth that whosoever here after shall make like
attempt or commit like offence, shall not escape with like
punishment.'

Soon after More had taken up office the King made known
his price for his favour. He asked More to weigh and consider
once again the matter of the divorce on which His Majesty's
heart was set. The Chancellor fell on his knees and entreated
the King to forgive him for his incapacity to help him. 'There
was nothing in the world had been so grievous to his heart, as
to remember he was not able, as he willingly would with the
loss of one of his limbs, for that matter to find anything whereby he could serve his Grace's contentment, as he that always
bare in mind the most godly words, that his Highness spake
unto him at his first coming into his noble service, the most

virtuous lesson that ever prince taught his servant, willing him first to look unto God, and after God to him, as in good faith he did, or else might his Grace well account him most unworthy servant.'

The King replied, no doubt huffily, to the man whose compliance he had so much hoped to win that 'if he could not with his conscience serve him, he was content to accept his service otherwise, and use the advice of other of his learned Council, whose consciences could well enough agree thereto, he would nevertheless continue his gracious favour towards him, and never with that matter molest his conscience after.'

We shall do well to look beyond the bare words of this story, to the irony of the King, to the tension which must have sprung up between the two men at that instant. The struggle between the two strongest wills in England had begun.

The Parliament before which More, as the mouthpiece of the King, condemned Wolsey, was described by More at his trial as 'God knoweth what manner of one'. It was England's reformation Parliament and lasted for seven years, and at its dissolution England was a changed nation. Whether that Parliament was a picked one, consisting of King's men, or simply of those who, sharing the hatreds and avarice of the King, were only too willing to go as far as possible with him, is still debated by historians. It need not concern us, for what it accomplished is not in question. The obedience to Rome was broken, the Church subordinated to the civil authority, the monasteries and hospitals plundered and dissolved, and the genius of England silenced. It was not a Parliament concerned with liberty, or aware of the spiritual heritage of Christendom, or of the peril involved in destroying it, but rather one of hard new men, 'jolly crackers and braggers', *bourgeois*, lawyers, enclosing squires. Thomas Cromwell, open disciple of Machiavelli, was its natural leader.

Henry treated his Parliament tenderly, nursing it along that it might be the more pliable in his hands. His first attack, how-

ever, was upon Parliament itself, and it was as preposterous as
it was cunning. By establishing a Legatine Court and trying
the King's case, Wolsey had exposed himself to the charge of
*praemunire*, which could be alleged against anyone presuming
to uphold the papal authority against the King's: the penalties
were forfeiture of land and goods, and imprisonment. But
Henry sought to lay the blame upon Parliament and the Church
for permitting Wolsey so to act, though Parliament was not
a sembled, and as though his own neglect to dismiss Wolsey
was the nation's fault. The Cardinal was a prelate and legate;
he was the leader of the Church in England; it was implied
therefore in the charge against the Church that it was specially
culpable and could not disclaim responsibility. The Convocations of Canterbury and York were compelled to pay a fine
totalling £119,000, and at the same time required to recognize
Henry as 'sole protector and supreme head of the Church and
clergy of England'. When the pardon of the King to the
Church was embodied in a parliamentary Bill, the Commons
took fright because they were not included, and resisted the
Bill. They were afraid exactions even greater would be laid
upon them, and Henry, who needed them against the Church,
yielded to their murmurings. The Church did not share in the
King's clemency. It had lost a million (in our money) and
independence. Yet no one in the country then imagined that
the Church's surrender was more than a snook cocked at the
Pope for his failure in the divorce. It was part of the squeeze,
like some of the bills presented to Parliament for church reform. If the Pope would not yield, it should be made very
clear to him what it was going to cost him. The hope of papal
approval was still alive, and if that were settled to the King's
satisfaction, the affairs of the Church might take on a new
turn. So must Thomas More have thought, who himself initiated reform measures. Nevertheless the proposal to milk the
Church and to make Henry supreme head, stuck in the throats
of the Convocations. Fisher, the courageous Bishop of Roches-

ter, who had spoken out in the King's Council against the divorce, and who had been reprimanded by Parliament for his contemptuous assessment of their anti-clerical motives, suggested a compromise. And as proposed by Archbishop Warham, and passed by the Convocation on 11th February 1531, it was an acknowledgement that the King was their singular protector, only and supreme lord, and even supreme head but only 'so far as the law of Christ allows'. All the same, it was an ignoble surrender, and Convocation knew it. When the words were submitted to the assembly, there was silence. 'Whoever is silent seems to consent,' the Archbishop warned them. 'Then we are all silent,' said one. And in this manner was the capitulation made.

Meanwhile the matter of the divorce proceeded. In March 1530, the Pope caused a bull to be fixed to the doors of the churches in Flanders warning Henry on pain of excommunication against proceeding with a second marriage. In the same year Thomas Cranmer had suggested the Gilbertian procedure of appealing to the universities of Europe for their views of the divorce. So political a matter immediately created factions and parties within the universities and the King's largesse was liberally scattered to sweeten the decisions of the learned. The discreditable business helped the King's cause in Rome not at all, but, of course, the more confirmed him in his decision to go his own way. When the replies of the several universities were received, the Lord Chancellor, Sir Thomas More, despite the King's promise not to use him in this matter, came down to Parliament to acquaint the members with the substance of them; he said:

'You of this worshipful house I am sure be not so ignorant but you know well that the king our sovereign lord hath married his brother's wife, for she was both wedded and bedded with his brother prince Arthur, and therefore you may surely say that he hath married his brother's wife; if this marriage be good or no many clerks do doubt. Wherefore the king like a virtuous prince willing to be satisfied in his conscience and also for the surety of his realm hath with great deliberation consulted with great clerks, and hath sent my Lord of London here present to the chief universities of All Christendom to know their opinion and judgment in that behalf. And although the universities of Cambridge and Oxford had been sufficient to discuss the cause, yet because they be in his realm and to avoid all suspicions of partiality he hath sent into the realm of France, Italy, the Pope's dominions, and Venetians to know their judgement in that behalf, which have concluded, written and sealed their determinations according as you shall hear read.' Then some twelve more or less favourable communications f om the universities were read to Parliament. More was asked for his opinion and replied that he had several times made it known to the King, a reply the guarded nature of which made all too clear his opposition. Indeed, More's resistance to those appetites of the King which Wolsey had been unable to restrain, was so well known that the Emperor Charles sought to communicate directly with him, and More had to refuse to receive his letters lest his loyalty to the King might be called in question, and any influence he might have left in the matter vanish overnight. After the hearing of the decisions of the universities Parliament was prorogued. Queen Katherine was acquainted with the proceedings, and asked whether she would now accept the decisions of a mixed commission of temporal and spiritual lords. She replied that she would abide by her appeal to the Court of Rome, and implied that the favourable verdict of the universities was corruptly procured. This was shortly before Whitsun, and within a few weeks the Queen was deprived of her royal estate. Anne Boleyn had triumphed.

Parliament met again the following year and renewed its attack on the Church under the inspiration of Thomas Cromwell. A Supplication of the Commons was made to the King against the power of ordinaries to summon men before their courts for heresy and other offences against the Church. But in this same Parliament in April 1532, one Temse spoke in the House of Commons against the separation of the King and Queen and the stigma of bastardy which now rested on the innocent Princess Mary. At this time, too, there was much murmuring about the favour enjoyed by Anne Boleyn; the common talk was that it was by her influence that the Queen had been expelled from the royal palaces. The King sent for the Speaker and explained his royal conscience once again. It was for conscience' sake that he had separated from the Queen; 'saving in Spain or Portugal it hath not been seen, that one man married two sisters, the one being carnally known before: but the brother to marry the brother's wife was so abhorred amongst all nations, that I never heard it, that any Christian man did it but myself.' At the same time the King with characteristic skill presented to the Speaker the replies of the Spirituality to the complaints of the Commons, remarking that he did not think they would please them, 'for it seemeth to us very slender'. However, look into the matter in your wisdom, and when that has been done the King will judge impartially in the quarrel!

The King lacked the patience to wait, and recalled the Speaker in May and revealed his new discovery. It was: 'We thought that the clergy of our realm, had been our subjects wholly, but now we have well perceived, that they be but half our subjects, yea, and scarce our subjects: for all the Prelates at their consecration make an oath to the Pope, clean contrary to the oath that they make to us, so that they seem to be his subjects, and not ours, the copy of both oaths I deliver here to you, requiring you to invent some order, that we be not thus deluded of our spiritual subjects.'

Parliament was dismissed on the 14th May. On the day after, Convocation surrendered all its rights to Henry. The independence of the Church was ended; the clergy were required to forswear the Pope and acknowledge that their authority came only from the King, and to promise not to legislate without it. With Bishop Gardiner, More had fought a delaying action on behalf of the Church, but the Convocation's capitulation left him isolated and helpless. On the 16th, 'after long suits to the King to be discharged of that office' More was permitted to hand back to the King the Great Seal of his office 'and was with the king's favour discharged'.

Warham, Archbishop of Canterbury, and scholar of the new learning, died in August 1532, saddened by these grievous events. Cranmer, the priest so officious in the King's divorce, was promoted to the See of Canterbury. In January 1533, Henry married Anne Boleyn secretly, and Cranmer's court obediently gave the King his divorce in the following May. Katherine, who refused to appear before the court, was declared contumacious. Seven days after the court's decision the woman Henry had secretly married before his divorce was crowned at Westminster by Cranmer. The matter was urgent, for a child was expected, the future Elizabeth. Sir Thomas More's prophetic comment to Roper was, 'God give grace, son, that these matters within a while be not confirmed with oaths'.

The coronation was celebrated with all the magnificence Henry enjoyed. The pert Anne could not have disliked it either. She was brought from Greenwich to the Tower by water in barges garnished with banners and streamers, and conveyed in the customary triumph from the Tower to Westminster. The streets were gravelled, and railed on one side, and the guildmen in their liveries lined the streets. The city constables, apparelled in velvet and silk, kept order, great staves in hand. Houses were hung with tapestries of scarlet, cloth of gold, carpets and rich arras. She, whom the French ambassador had called the King's *amie* was conveyed in a litter of cloth of gold drawn by palfries clad in white damask. Over her was borne a canopy of cloth of gold with four gilt statues and four silver bells. The procession wound through the glittering streets, past fountains running with Rhenish wine and under triumphal arches. But one man

THE GREAT DIVORCE

was missing in her train. Whether he would attend or not must have been the gossip of London. The friends and allies of More, Cuthbert Tunstall, Bishop of Durham; Gardiner, Bishop of Winchester; and Clerk, Bishop of Bath, knowing of his poverty and peril, sent More £20 to buy a gown with the request that he should accompany them from the Tower to Westminster for the coronation. More accepted the £20, but stayed at home, and when next he met his friends greeted them with raillery: 'My Lords, in the letters you late sent me, you required two things of me, the one whereof since I was so well contented to grant you, the other therefore I thought I might be the bolder to deny you.'

Malicious eyes must have searched the cavalcade and noted the absence of the most famous citizen of London. It was a plain and open rebuke to the royal tyrant from the man who had till recently enjoyed the highest office in the land, and it could not be overlooked. What followed after was persecution.

Sir Thomas More, who had behaved with the subtlest discretion over his resignation, perhaps hoped that his absence might not be overmuch resented, but put down to the infirmities which had been growing upon him. He was suffering badly from bronchial troubles and made this his principal justification in the letter to Erasmus which explained his surrender of the high office:

'From the time I was a boy I have longed, dear Desiderius, that what I rejoice in you always having enjoyed I myself might some day also enjoy—namely, that being free from public business, I might also have some time to devote to God and myself; that, by the grace of a great and good God, and by the favour of an indulgent prince, I have at least obtained. I have not, however, obtained it as I wished. For I wished to reach that last stage of my life in a state, which, though suitable to my age, might yet enable me to enjoy my remaining years healthy and unbroken, free from disease and pain. But it remains in the hands of God whether this wish, perhaps unreasonable, shall be

accomplished. Meanwhile a disorder of I know not what nature
has attacked my chest, by which I suffer less in present pain
than in fear of the consequence. For when it had plagued me
without abatement some months, the physicians whom I consulted gave their opinion that the long continuance of it was
dangerous, and speedy cure impossible; but that it must be
cured by the gradual alternative effects of time, proper diet,
and medicine. Neither could they fix the period of my recovery
nor ensure me a complete cure at last. Considering this, I saw
that I must either lay down my office or discharge my duty in
it incompletely. . . .'²

This letter was dated from Chelsea, 14th June 1532. It was
delayed in reaching Erasmus who, unprompted, had to defend
his friend from the rumours circulating on the Continent. One,
holding More responsible for the bitter persecution of heretics,
declared that More's successor Audley had flung open all the
jails and released all those imprisoned for their beliefs. Erasmus
vindicated More with great spirit, declaring that he was a
gentle soul who had never been known to persecute heretics,
but was most willing to let them alone if only they would
abandon their sectarian principles. In any case, he argued, what
point was there in trying to blacken More over this when it
was well known that the King of England himself was far less
tolerant of the new doctrines than bishops and priests. Erasmus
went on to speak of a family tomb constructed by More in the
Chelsea village church over which More himself had placed
an epitaph telling his life story. This is the slab I mentioned as
having survived the German bombing. The epitaph is important for the very reason that More prepared it against the day
when his reputation might be blackened. It is his justification,
meant to give his own estimate of his worth to posterity. In it
More lists the offices he has held—under-sheriff of London,
made a member of the King's Council, and a knight, then
under-treasurer, Chancellor of the Duchy of Lancaster, and
finally Lord Chancellor of England. He speaks of his embassies

and praises his colleagues who shared them with him. Then comes a very personal note:

'When he had thus gone through this course of offices or honours, that neither that gracious prince could disallow his doings, nor was he odious to the nobility nor unpleasant to the people, but yet to thieves, murderers and heretics grievous, at last John More, his father, knight, and chosen of the prince to be one of the justices of the King's Bench, a civil man, pleasant, harmless, gentle, pitiful, just and uncorrupted, in years old, but in body more than for his years lusty, after that he perceived his life so long lengthened, that he saw his son Lord Chancellor of England, thinking himself now to have lived long enough, gladly departed to God. His son then, his father being dead, to whom as long as he lived being compared was wont both to be called young and himself thought so, too, missing now his father departed, and seeing four children of his own, and of their offspring eleven, began in his own conceit to wax old; and this affection of his was increased by a certain sickly disposition of his breast, even by and by following, as a sign or token of age creeping upon him. He therefore, irked and weary of worldly business, giving up his promotions, obtained at last by the incomparable benefit of his most gentle prince, if it pleases God to favour his enterprise, the thing which from a child in a manner he always wished and desired: that he might have some years of his life free, in which he little and little withdrawing himself from the business of this life, might continually remember the immortality of the life to come.'[3]

This was also sent to Erasmus for publication, that More might defend his reputation in Europe. He did not approve of what the King had done, but he would not contend with him, form any faction, or lend his name to any movement against the King either in England or Europe. The spirit of the epitaph and of letters to friends was the decision 'not to meddle more in worldly matters'.

When More retired into poverty he placed all his gentlemen

and yeomen with bishops and noblemen, and his watermen with Audley, his successor in office, to whom he also passed on his official barge, and called his children together and told them of the new situation, and that economy was now imperative. He asked for their advice, but they were silent, more shattered than he by the blow. 'Then will I show my poor mind to you,' he said, according to Roper. 'I have been brought up at Oxford, at an Inn of Chancery, at Lincoln's Inn, and in the King's Court, so forth from the lowest degree to the highest, and yet have I in yearly revenues little more than one hundred pounds by the year at this present left me. So that now we must hereafter, if we like to live together, be contented to become contributaries together. But by my counsel it shall not be best for us to fall to the lowest fare first. We will not therefore descend to Oxford fare, nor to the fare of New Inn, but we will begin with Lincoln's Inn diet, where many right worshipful and of good years do live full well, which if we find not ourselves the first year able to maintain, then will we the next year after go one step down to New Inn fare, wherewith many an honest man is well contented. If that exceed our ability, too, then will we the next year after descend to Oxford fare, where many grave, ancient, and learned Fathers be conversant continually, which if our ability stretch not to maintain neither, then may we yet with bags and wallets go a-begging together, and hoping that for pity some good folks will give their charity at every man's door to sing *salve Regina*, and so still keep company merrily together.'

The spirits were high, but the poverty was real, and on cold nights piles of bracken had to be brought in and burnt in the bedroom fireplaces to heat the rooms, for of other fuel there was none.

# CHAPTER TEN

# 'TREADING HERETICS LIKE ANTS'

A great collection was made by the Church to reward More for his many works against heresy. According to Roper it amounted to four to five thousand pounds. Despite the admonitions of his friends that if he could not take it for himself, at least he ought to take it for the sake of his wife and children, who now suffered from the poverty his resignation had brought, the obstinate man utterly refused it, saying that he would sooner see it cast into the Thames than he or any of his have one penny of it. Indeed, he asserted that he regarded his works against heresy, however necessary, as so much loss of sleep as far as he was concerned; he would prefer, so that heresies were suppressed, that all his books were burned and his labour utterly lost. He had no wish that people should read either heretics' books or his own; they should occupy themselves with real books of devotion like the *Imitation of Christ*.

The spread of the Lutheran heresy in Germany and the Low Countries exercised a deep and lasting effect on More's England. Roper's fall from grace is evidence enough of how the new doctrines spread from the German merchants in the city into the most unlikely quarters, and Strype, in his *Ecclesiastical Memorials*, informs us that Tyndale's heretical views even reached and influenced the King. In 1528 two works of Tyndale appeared, *The Parable of Wicked Mammon*, which treats of justification by faith, and *The Obedience of a Christian Man*, a powerful work which proposes the abolition of the authority of the Church in favour of that of the Bible and effectively replies to the argument that the Reformers preached civil disobedience by demanding the absolute submission to earthly princes. Wolsey was seeking, as a matter of policy, to keep Lutheran and heretical works out of the way of the King, fearing lest they might provide a handle for the anti-clerical party in which Rochfort and Anne Boleyn were prominent. Among the ladies-in-waiting of Anne Boleyn was a young gentlewoman called Mistress Gainford who was being courted by a Mr. George Zouch. In their loving play he snatched a book she was reading, and would not return it. It happened to be Tyndale's *The Obedience of a Christian Man*, lent to her by Anne Boleyn. Zouch became so engrossed in this work that he read it at all hours, however unseasonable, and Mistress Gainford was enraged because she could not secure its return. It happened that Dr. Sampson, Dean of the King's Chapel, one who served on embassies with More, happened to catch sight of the book which Zouch was reading in his presence. He confiscated it, and delivered it to the Cardinal, as he had been instructed to do with all heretical literature found in the court. The loss was reported to Anne Boleyn, who said, 'Well, it shall be the dearest book that ever Dean or Cardinal took away'. And forthwith went to the King who caused the book to be restored. Then she brought it to the King to read. And this he did, commenting afterwards with delight, 'This is the book for me and all kings to read'. And well might he say so.

Yet despite this, the King was no heretic in the Lutheran sense; we may more justly describe him as a schismatic. He made no quarrel with Rome over doctrine, and rejected the blandishments of the Lutherans. The Church remained for him the sacramental church; if it was not to be the Roman Church, it would become the English Church, never a private one in which any Tom, Dick or Harry could make doctrine. What he was proposing was merely the termination of the Pope's authority over his own domains; the Church was to remain in other respects the same Church. And that explains why Henry was more zealous to persecute heretics after the break with

Rome than before. This also makes it easier to understand why the King who defended papal authority with much skill in his *Assertation of the Seven Sacraments*, written in direct reply to Luther's *Babylonian Captivity*, became himself one of the destroyers of that authority.

The King's book was finished in 1521, only seven years before Tyndale's *Obedience*, and in his letter presenting it to Leo, Henry wrote that ever since he had learnt of Luther's heresy in Germany, 'he had made it his study how to extirpate it. He had called the learned of his kingdom to consider these errors and denounce them, and exhort others to do the same. He had urged the Emperor and Electors, since this pestilent fellow would not return to God, to extirpate him and his heretical books. He thought it right still further to testify his zeal for the faith by his writings, that all might see he was ready to defend the Church, not only with his arms, but with the resources of his mind. He dedicated therefore, to the Pope, the first offerings of his intellect and his little erudition.' And to mark the importance of the work which gained him the title of 'Defender of the Faith' Luther's books were burnt at Paul's Cross in Wolsey's presence, while Bishop Fisher preached a sermon against them.

Where the sovereign advanced into the fray it was not for the servant to show sloth. And More was indeed one of 'the learned of the kingdom' called to the denunciation of error. And he saw no cause to halt because the King became involved in perils to his soul and conflict with Rome over the divorce. The great landmark in the advance of Protestant thinking in England was the publication of Tyndale's New Testament in 1525. It was, in the manner of its translation, a clear declaration of allegiance to Lutheranism. When copies of it began to circulate in London, Cuthbert Tunstall, then Bishop of London, bought them up and had them burnt. And when on one occasion Thomas More was examining a heretic and inquired about the finances of Tyndale, he received the reply: 'Marry, it is the Bishop of London that hath holpen us, for he hath bestowed among us a great deal of money in New Testaments to burn them, and that hath been and yet is our only succour and comfort.' More replied: 'Now, by my troth, I think even the same; and I said so much to the Bishop, when he went about to buy them.'

In 1528, before he was Chancellor, that is, More produced the first of his great works against heresy in *Dialogue Concerning Heresies*, an answer both to Luther and Tyndale. To Simon Fish's shrewd propaganda against the wealth of the Church, *Supplication for the Beggars*, which urged the confiscation of church property, More replied with *Supplication of Souls* (1529). During his Chancellorship More continued to reply to Tyndale with a *Confutation of Tyndale's Answer*, which he completed on his retirement. There were several other works, and many letters, which carried on, in season and out, the relentless debate.

In *Dialogue Concerning Heresies* More was at pains to explain that there was no hostility on the part of the Church to translations of the Scriptures as such. Many had been made in the past, even long before Wyclif's days. He himself had seen many such Bibles fairly and reverently translated and left in the hands of laymen. But they were authorized. It was the unauthorized translation which the Church condemned, for the simple reason that it could easily become the vehicle of heresy, or misunderstanding. In matters of the Scriptures, which touched the heart of the Christian life, it was not for one man in his translation to set himself up as equal in authority to the whole Church. Erasmus had pleaded for translations into the vernacular and More remained of the same opinion he had been at the time of Erasmus's translation of the Greek Testament in 1515, that this was a necessary step, and that the fear which some clergy had of it 'nothing feareth me; but whosoever would of their malice and folly take harm of that thing that is of itself ordained to do all men good, I would never, for the avoiding of their harm, take from other the profit which they

might take, and nothing deserve to lose. For else, if the abuse
of a good thing should cause the taking away thereof from other
than would use it well, Christ himself have never been born.'[1]

More, the King's and the nation's spokesman, goes farther.
His Majesty is, he says, of his blessed zeal, about to act to procure an authorized version, and the wishes of the people will
therefore be satisfied. (Twelve years later the King authorized
a version; it was, with some corrections, Tyndale's.)

*Dialogue Concerning Heresies* is cast in the form of a discussion
with a messenger sent by a friend who wanted advice about
current heresies. It is altogether a lively and readable debate.
In the eighth chapter More sets out his objections to Tyndale's
translations in passages justifying the burning of the Testament. He strives to show how Tyndale has distorted the meaning of the Scriptures and 'corrupted and changed it [the New
Testament] from the good and wholesome doctrine of Christ
to the devillish heresies of their [the Lutherans'] own'. It is a
scholarly attack. Tyndale 'hath mistranslated three words of
great weight and every one of them is, as I suppose, more than
thrice three times repeated in the book. . . . The one is . . . this
word (priests). The other the Church. The third Charity. For
Priests whereso ever he speaketh of the Priests of Christ's
Church, he never calleth them Priests, but always Seniors. The
Church he calleth the congregation, and Charity he calleth
love. Now do these names in our English tongue neither express the things that he meant by them, and also there appeareth
(the circumstances well considered) that he had a mischievous
mind in the change.

'For first, as for priests and priesthood, though that of old
they used commonly to choose well elderly men to be priests,
and therefore in the Greek tongue priests were called *presbiteri*,
as we might say, elder men; yet neither were all priests chosen
old, as appeareth by Saint Paul writing to Tymotheus, *Nemo
juventutem tuam contemnat*. Let no man contemn thy youth, nor
every elder man is not a priest.' The word 'senior', More as-

serts, means almost nothing in the English language; it's a French word used mockingly, or else it is used to signify someone like an alderman. What Tyndale is plainly determined to do is to use any word *but* 'priest', and for the obvious reason that Lutherans hate the priestly office. 'Now where he calleth the church alway the *congregation*, what reason had he therein? For every man well seeth that though the church be indeed a congregation, yet is not every congregation the church . . . which is a word common to a company of christian men or a company of Turks.' Tyndale also coarsens the meaning of the Scriptures by dropping the word 'charity' and using 'love' instead, so that it may become impossible to distinguish between holy and virtuous affection and the 'lewd love that is between a flecke and his make'. And for the same Lutheran heresy which asserts that 'all our salvation standeth in faith alone', and good works contribute nothing, Tyndale translated *grace* as *favour*, *confession* as *knowledge*, *penance* as *repentance*, *a contrite heart* as *a troubled heart*.

From a discussion of Tyndale's New Testament More passed on to a consideration of the general Lutheran position, and he made in one place that oft-quoted, and most charitable defence of the much-abused sixteenth-century clergy: 'If they be familiar, we call them light. If they be solitary, we call them fantastic. If they be sad, we call them solemn. If they be merry, we call them mad. If they be companionable we call them vicious. If they be holy we call them hypocrites. If they keep few servants we call them niggards. If they keep many we call them pompous. If a lewd priest do a lewd deed, then we say, lo, see what sample the clergy giveth us, as though the priest were the clergy. But then forget we to look what good men be therein, and what good counsel they give us, and what good ensample they show us. But we fare as do the ravens and the carrion crows that never meddle with any quick flesh; but where they may find a dead dog in a ditch, thereto they flee and thereupon they feed apace.'[2]

More cannot forbear to point out that Luther discounts the role of reason: 'and as for reason, he refused to stand to, saying that the matters of our faith be things above reason and that reason hindereth us in our faith, and is unto faith an enemy.' Once again More declares against the supremacy of private judgment, which was so vital an issue with him. 'The church hath always taught against the putting of a proud trust in our own deeds because that we cannot alway surely judge our own deeds for the blind favour that we bear toward ourself.' When Luther answered Henry's *Seven Sacraments* in a work which contained much abuse, More replied in Latin as polemical, but under the pseudonym of William Ross, described as an Englishman but recently returned from a trip to Italy. Father T. E. Bridgett, the great biographer of More, translated passages of Luther and More and set them side by side in order to show the drift of their thought. I borrow representative passages on private judgment, for these are at the root not only of More's general defence of the Church, but of his particular quarrel with Henry VIII.

*Words of Luther:* 'It is written, "All things are yours, whether Apollo or Cephas or Paul, and you are Christ's" (1 Cor. iii. 22). If we are Christ's only, who is this stupid king, who strives with his lies to make us the Pope's? We are not the Pope's, but the Pope is ours. It is ours, not to be judged by the Pope, but to judge him. "For the spiritual man is judged by none, but he judges all men" (omnes) (1 Cor. ii. 15). If it is true that all things are yours, even the Pope, how much more that dirt and disgrace of men, the Thomists and Henricians?'

*Words of More:* 'May I die if frenzy itself is so frenetical, or madness itself so mad, as this waggish head of Luther's. The Pope is ours, he says; therefore it is ours to judge him, not to be judged by him. By the same reasoning: The physician is ours, therefore it is ours to cure him, not to be cured by him; and the schoolmaster belongs to the scholars, therefore it belongs to them to teach him, and not to learn from him!

# 'TREADING HERETICS LIKE ANTS'

'It is ours, he says, not to be judged by the Pope, but to judge him. What does he mean by "ours"? Does he mean "of the whole" collectively, or "of each one" in particular? If he means "of the whole", he advances nothing for himself, since the whole of the Church is for the Pope, and against Luther. And in the matter of the sacraments still less, since people and Pope, both present and past, are in favour of the sacraments, and against Luther. But if it belongs to each one to judge the Pope and the sacraments, and the true sense of Scripture—since, among so many judges, the judgment of Luther alone is on one side—by what prerogative must his vote outweigh the votes of all the rest? Because, he says, the spiritual man judges all, and he is judged by none; and because "all things are yours, even the Pope". Reader, do you not seem to be listening to raving? Luther alone is spiritual; the Pope alone is unspiritual; so Luther must judge all and be judged by none, and the Pope must judge none, and be judged by all! And this raver does not see that, while he is raving against the Pope, he is raving also against Peter and Paul. For when the Apostle said "all things are yours," he did not add "the Pope", but Apollo, Cephas, and Paul. Hence Luther must reason consistently: We are not Peter's or Paul's, but Peter and Paul are ours; therefore it is ours to judge Peter and Paul, and not to be judged by them. Nay, not so much ours as "mine", for it is the prerogative of the spiritual man to judge and not be judged. Hence the spiritual man, Luther, shall judge, not Thomists and Henricians only, but Peter and Paul and the rest of the Apostles.'[3]

These passages do not do justice to Luther's thought, but that is not the task of this book. They do, however, reveal the mind of More. It is frequently possible to substitute "Henry" for "Luther" in the passage above, for Henry had convinced himself that he was the proper judge of the issues of the divorce, as Luther had convinced himself that he was a proper judge of the issues of the Church. Their defiance of the Pope has points of resemblance. Henry instructed his ambassador to communi-

cate to Charles in 1533 his conviction that he had been living
in incestuous union with his brother's wife, and that 'The justice of our cause is so rooted in our breast that nothing can remove it, and even the canons say that a man should rather en-
dure all the censures of the Church than offend his conscience'.
Of like import is the message he sent to the Lutheran princes in
1534 to the effect that he believed that a man's conscience was
the highest and most supreme court of justice.

Thomas More was not always a shining light of courtesy in
the controversies in which he indulged for the sake of the King
or the Church; matters were too urgent, his opponents too
rough for niceties; but he *was* consistent. The Bible was not one
thing and the Church another, the Bible not infallible and the
Church fallible. The Christian man not all incorruptible spirit,
and his Church all corruption! The Bible, in the manner in
which it reached men, was the work of men and one had only
to look at their translations to see what were the possibilities of
error. No, Bible and Church were one inheritance, not to be
opposed to each other, but to be understood and used together.
To Christianity the continuity of doctrine, teaching, interpretation, and law were as important as the physical continuity
of the laying-on of hands. Standing over the individual Christian conscience was the accumulated wisdom of the General
Council of Christendom in which the dead as well as the living
were to be numbered. It was not for a man to smother his conscience, but to conform it to the Christian norm, to hold his
views not with all the arrogance and pride of individualism,
but under advice and counsel from the Church through the ages.

It remains only to be said that the once popular view that
More was a persecutor of heretics has been proved false in our
day. The authorities cannot find the evidence that this was so,
despite the allegations of Edward Hall and others. Professor
R. W. Chambers has disposed of this blot on More's memory:
he has shown that during the twelve years, including More's
period as Chancellor, during which More waged war against

heretics, 'not one death sentence [was] pronounced on a heretic in the diocese of London'. The Smithfield fires were lit again only after the King had assumed the title of Supreme Head—in February 1531—when More 'though still in office, was no longer in power'. The same scholar has even shown how More has been misrepresented down the centuries through the bowdlerization of a passage in his *Apology*. The effect of the mutilation of More's statement made it appear that he had flogged a half-wit for heresy. But the unexpurgated text, which Chambers restores, makes it clear that the man was flogged for indecent assaults on women during Mass. All the evidence we have of More's activities tends to confirm that he was in public life what he was in his Chelsea home, gentle but unyielding in the right. He was courtesy itself to visiting German heretics, and as with Roper, he preferred to argue, confute, persuade, pray, rather than punish. We do well to recall, however, that his fear of heresy sprang from civil as well as religious apprehensions. He was long a member of the Government, then Lord Chancellor; and at all times deeply concerned with the peace of the realm. The examples of Germany, Rome, and the Turkish invasion were constantly before him. He knew that heresy sooner or later was associated with brawl and disturbance. It was a seed-bed of rebellion against all authority, and a cause of war. Hence, as he sought to show in *Dialogue Concerning Heresies*, the temporal power was justified in putting down heretics with a strong hand: it had the right to burn them. The pages of *Utopia* reveal the same horror of civil dissension and the same belief in strong measures against it. One needs only to read his account of the Sack of Rome, hardly printable to-day, to understand what his feelings were. Finally, we must recognize that his fear for Europe was prophetic, for the triumph of the Reformation led to a century of religious wars and persecutions which stained Christianity with unspeakable crimes, and inflicted upon a despairing continent what Hitler and Stalin have in our day inflicted on our Europe.

# CHAPTER ELEVEN

# THE PERSECUTION

A contest of wits and wills opened between the King and his Council and the wary More. Towards the end of 1533 the Council caused a proclamation to be made in which the King's marriage was defended. It argued that Cranmer's judgment was founded on the decisions of the universities of Europe, supported by the pleas of the entire clergy. It asserted that causes ought never to be removed from the country in which they were begun, for otherwise, for instance, the inheritance of this realm could be made to depend on the decisions of 'the Bishop of Rome, by some men called the Pope'. The General Council, it held, was superior to all bishops, including the Bishop of Rome, and any man, let alone a prince, could appeal from the Pope's decisions to the Council. The last article of this defence consisted of the kind of abuse all too familiar in the religious controversies of the century: it accused the Pope of being himself a bastard, simoniac and heretic.

A pamphlet appeared in answer to the royal justification, and More was thought to be the author and William Rastell, his nephew, the printer and publisher. Rastell was brought before the Council. He denied all knowledge of the book, and nothing could be proved against him. More sniffed the new wind blowing, and thought it judicious to follow up the indirect accusation by direct denial to Thomas Cromwell, then secretary to the King, arguing in his disclaimer that, as to the proclamation of the Council concerning the King's marriage, he could not have made an answer 'for of the many things which in that book be touched, in some I know not the law, and in some I know not the fact'. But above and beyond such considerations he asked the Council whether they really thought he was the sort of man secretly to make such a reply, or to cause or advise others to do so.

Other stratagems were resorted to. Roper reports, with his customary brilliance, an effort to accuse More retrospectively of corrupt practices while Chancellor. One Parnell, who had received an adverse verdict from More, now complained to the King that it was a corrupt one, because More had received a bribe from his adversary in the case, Vaughan. This Vaughan, unable to go abroad because of the gout, had 'by the hands of his wife' presented More with a great gilt cup. More, 'thereupon by the King's appointment being called before the Council, where that matter was heinous laid to his charge, forthwith confessed, that forasmuch as that cup was long after the aforesaid decree brought unto him for a new year's gift, he upon her importunate pressing upon him, therefore of courtesy refused not to take it. Then the Lord of Wiltshire (for hatred of his religion preferrer of this suit) with much rejoicing said unto the Lords, "Lo, my Lords, lo, did I not tell you that you should find this matter true?" Where upon Sir Thomas More desired their worships, that as they courteously heard him tell the one part of his tale, so they would vouchsafe of their honours indifferently to hear the other, after which he obtained, he further declared unto them, that albeit indeed he had with much work received that cup, yet immediately thereupon he caused his butler to fill that with wine, and of that cup drank to her, and that when she had pledged him, then as freely as her husband had given it unto him, even so freely gave he the same unto her again, to give unto her husband for his new year's gift, which at his instant request, though much against her will, yet at length she was fain to receive.' And upon being called before the Council, Mrs. Vaughan deposed to the truth of this. 'Thus', Roper writes triumphantly, 'was the great mountain turned scarce into a molehill.'

Nothing came of this first effort to blacken More. But the malevolence was unremitting, and no sooner were these matters disposed of than other opportunities presented themselves. A Kentish kitchen maid, Elizabeth Barton, in her youth a victim of epilepsy, and said to have been cured of it by the good offices of Our Lady, became a nun of Canterbury and gained fame as the Holy Maid of Kent. In trances she prophesied and made revelations, and the populace resorted to her. One has to understand that to the medieval mind it did not appear impossible that God should use such a maid for his revelations, which explains the willingness of Carthusians and Franciscans, and of Thomas More and Bishop Fisher, yes and even Wolsey and the King, to have traffic with her. The indefatigable Hall wrote that, about the time of the christening of Princess Elizabeth ,'was espied a new found saint, and holy hypocrite, called the Maid of Kent, which by the great labour, diligence, and pain of the Archbishop of Canterbury, and the Lord Cromwell, and one called Hugh Latimer, a priest (which shortly after was made bishop of Worcester), the juggling and crafty deceit of this maid, was manifested and brought to light: whereupon after diverse examinations, she with all her adherents, were in November brought to the star chamber.' The Maid's revelations had included threats of divine retribution against the King should he persist in the divorce. In pursuit of this political mission the maid had approached even Henry himself in years past. In the dangerous times of which we are speaking her claim to pronounce with divine authority about the marriage became an embarrassment to Henry and a source of satisfaction to the opponents of the Boleyn faction. The Maid was executed, with many of those who had listened to her, in April 1534. Among those she had seriously compromised was Bishop Fisher of Rochester. In the course of the enquiries the name of Thomas More was mentioned by a Franciscan, Father Rich.

He stated that he had shown various revelations of the Maid to Sir Thomas, who had refused to listen to any concerning the King. The intention of Cromwell to embroil More now became plain, for despite the fact that Rich's evidence acquitted More of 'misprision of treason' Cromwell suppressed it, and reported to the King that More was among those who had listened to the Maid.

More made a long defence of his actions to Cromwell. He explained that he had first heard of the girl some eight or nine years before, when the Archbishop of Canterbury sent to the King an account of various things she had spoken in her trances. More related that the King had asked him to report on them, and though in matters religious he did not presume to judge, he had to declare to the King that he found nothing of any weight in the Maid's revelations. Nor, he said, did the King either. About a year later, More wrote, a certain Father Risby reported to him about the Maid, and of her warnings to Wolsey, but he refused to listen to any matters which concerned the King. Father Rich also spoke about her, but once again More rejected any talk which concerned the honour or policies of the King. Nevertheless (and, one must conclude, somewhat rashly, in view of the tenor of the Maid's rebukes to the King) More did see her alone in a little chapel at Sion and talked with her, but only of religious matters; 'we talked no words of the king's Grace.' He sent Cromwell a copy of the letter he had felt minded to write to the Maid after that visit. The germane part of it consisted of this warning: 'Good madam, I doubt not but that you remember that in the beginning of my communication with you I showed you that I neither was, nor would be, curious of any knowledge of other men's matters, and least of all of any matter of princes, or of the realm, in case it so were that God had, as to many good folks beforetime He hath, any time revealed unto you such things; I said unto your ladyship, that I was not only not desirous to hear of, but also would not hear of. Now, madam, I consider well that many folk desire to speak with you which are not all peradventure of my mind in this point; but some hap to be curious and inquisitive of things that little pertain to their parts; and some might peradventure hap to talk of such things as might after turn to much harm; as I think you have heard how the late Duke of Buckingham, moved with the fame of one that was reported for an holy monk, and had such talking with him, as after was a great part of his destruction, and disheriting of his blood, and great slander and infamy of religion.[1] It sufficeth me, good madam, to put you in remembrance of such things as I nothing doubt your wisdom and the Spirit of God shall keep you from talking with any persons, specially lay persons, of any such manner things as pertain to princes' affairs, or the state of the realm, but only to commune and talk with any person high and low of such manner things as may to the soul be profitable for you to show, and for them to know.'[2]

More told Cromwell that he had advised Father Rich not to accept what she spoke or preached as part of the faith, but even though good things might be done of her, to have all that she said or did most carefully examined by those with ecclesiastical authority over her, lest it should happen that her strange tales should prove false ones, and the Church suffer damage. More's own testimony was supported by the evidence of one of the accused friars, Rich or Risby, who told in writing what he remembered of More's letter to the Maid. Cromwell suppressed this, too. He was interested in the destruction of More, not in justice. In February 1534 a bill of attainder for misprision of treason was brought in Parliament against More and others for their relationship with the nun. More protested to Cromwell and appealed to the King to fulfil the promise he had made to More upon his retirement to grant him royal protection in any attack that might be made upon the honour of his conduct while in the service of the King.

Roper tells us that the King permitted More's name to go in the Bill in order to bring pressure upon him over more important matters, 'wherein his Grace was much deceived'. But not liking that More should appear before Parliament to make his own defence, the King appointed a commission consisting of the Archbishop of Canterbury, the Lord Chancellor Audley, the Duke of Norfolk, and Mr. Cromwell to examine him. Roper pleaded with More to secure the aid of these powerful men to get his discharge out of the Parliament Bill, and More replied that he would try. But when More met the commission, the intent of the whole matter was revealed. The petty business of the nun was forgotten. The Lord Chancellor declared that the King had showered many favours upon More, and that there was no honour he might not ask of him if only he would conform to the King's will (about the divorce and the supremacy). More replied that no man living knew better than he the extent of his debt to the King. 'Howbeit I verily hoped that I should never have heard of this matter more, considering that I have from time to time always from the beginning so plainly and truly declared my mind unto his Grace, which his Highness to me ever seemed, like a most gracious prince, very well to accept, never minding, as he said, to molest me more therefore. Since which time any further thing that was able to move me to any change I could never find, and if I could, there is none in all the world that could have been gladder of it than I.'

When the commission found that he could not be moved by their persuasions, they turned to the basest of threats. His ingratitude was vile: 'never was there servant to his master so villainous, nor subject to his prince so traitorous' as he. And in particular, he had by 'subtle sinister sleights' provoked the King to write his *Assertion of the Seven Sacraments* which had dishonoured the King throughout Christendom and put a sword into the Pope's hand against him. More's scornful answer was:

'These terrors be the arguments for children, and not for me. But to answer that wherewith you do chiefly burden me, I believe the King's Highness of his honour will never lay that to my charge. For none is there that in that point can say more in mine excuse than his Highness himself, who right well knoweth that I was never procurer or councillor of his Majesty thereunto, but after that it was finished, by his Grace's appointment, and consent of the makers of the same, only a sorter out, and placer of the principal matters therein contained; wherein when I found the Pope's authority highly advanced, and with strong arguments mightily defended, I said unto his Grace, I must put your Grace in remembrance of one thing, and that is this, The Pope (as your Grace knoweth) is a Prince as you are, and in league with all other Christian Princes; it may hereafter so fall out, that your Grace and he may vary upon some point of the league, whereupon may grow some breach of amity and war between you both; I think it best therefore that that place be amended, and his authority more slenderly touched. Nay (quoth his Grace) that it shall not, we are so much bounded unto the See of Rome, that we cannot do too much honour unto it. Then did I put him further in remembrance of Praemunire, whereby a good part of the Pope's pastoral cure here was paid away. To that answered his Highness, whatsoever impediment be to the contrary, we will set forth his authority to the uttermost. For we received from that See our Crown Imperial; which till his Grace with his own mouth told me I never heard before. So that I trust when his Grace shall be truly informed of this, and call to his gracious remembrance of my doings in that behalf, his Highness will never speak of it more, but clear me thoroughly therein.'

The dishonourable charge could not be maintained, and in an atmosphere of ill will the Commissioners allowed More to withdraw. The further charge of misprision of treason in connection with the Maid was also difficult to sustain. If More was to be charged, he was entitled to be heard in his defence, and it was a defence which, given his gifts, might have shaken the King's prestige grievously. And so, in the end, More's name was dropped from the Bill. But on his way home from the tussle with the Commissioners, More did not know that this was to be the outcome. Roper met him, and assumed from his father-in-law's high spirits that he had achieved his aim and 'gotten himself discharged out of the Parliament Bill'. As they walked in the Chelsea garden together he said to More: 'Sir, I trust all is well, because you are so merry.' 'That is so, indeed, son Roper, I thank God.' 'Are you put out of the Parliament Bill then?' 'By my troth, son Roper, I never remembered it.' 'Never remembered it, sir? A case that toucheth yourself so near, and us all for your sake! I am sorry to hear it. For I verily trusted when I saw you be so merry, that all had been well.' 'Wilt thou know, son Roper, why I was so merry?' 'That I would gladly, Sir.' 'In faith I rejoice, son, that I had given the devil so foul a fall, and that with those Lords I had gone so far, as, without great shame, I could never go back again.'

At which confession, Roper was downcast. But when he met Thomas Cromwell in Parliament and was told by him that More's name was dropped from the Bill, he sent the news home in haste to More by Margaret Roper. More was not impressed. What is deferred, he told Margaret, is not averted.

Immediately after his interview with the Council, Thomas More wrote a cool and well-reasoned letter[3] to Cromwell in which he set down his replies on the matters on which he had been examined. It was the sort of letter which allowed him hereafter no escape, consonant with his honour, from the position he had taken up; there is no doubt that he wrote it for that reason. He had been examined and had, in a sense, come off best from that encounter. But it would enrage the King, and those who had already capitulated to him, and the pressure would increase. Hence it was best to set down the position from which he did not intend to retreat, come what might.

In this historic letter he spoke of the primacy of the Pope as a matter upon which he had once been of the mind that it was not begun by the institution of God, 'until' (oh subtle answer!)

'that I read in that matter those things which the King's Highness had written in his most famous book against the heresies of Martin Luther. . . . But surely after that I read his Grace's book therein, and so many other things . . . these ten years since . . .' and looked into the works of all the holy doctors down to his own time, he had found that both the doctors and the general councils of the Church so agree with the King's book in this point, that he never found anything which would quiet his own conscience but rather put it in great peril 'if I should follow the other side, and deny the primacy to be provided by God'. Nor, he goes on, could he see anything to be gained by such a denial, for without the primacy, Christendom would be headless. 'And, therefore, since all Christendom is one corps, I cannot perceive how any member thereof may, without the common consent of the body, depart from the common head.' And if that is the case it becomes almost a matter of indifference from the practical point of view whether the primacy was instituted by the Church or ordained by God.

On the matter of the General Council, More embarks on the warning that the King was in fact appealing against the Pope *to* the General Council, but was proceeding in such a manner as to reject the General Council equally with the Pope. Diplomatically, he hopes this is not intended, for, he points out, the General Council might possibly depose the Pope and appoint one more to the King's liking. And the implication was, of course, that a General Council the authority of which the King had already rejected was hardly likely to bear on his side.

Urbane though the language is, the criticism of the King's policy is deadly. From it we can glean what More must often have said to the King in private. But whereas More in the first year of his retirement ventured neither criticism nor opinion, he emerged now, through the interview and the letter confirming it, as a public figure again, the leader of the spiritual opposition. The tenor of his views must soon have been bruited abroad. Imperturbable in manner, but merciless in logic, what

174

a formidable figure he must have appeared just then to King, Council and people!

A dangerous figure, even! Witness what the historian Pollard wrote of the position in England after the excommunication of 11th July 1533. 'Pope and Emperor were defied; Europe was shocked; Francis himself disapproved the breach with the Church; Ireland was in revolt; Scotland, as ever, was hostile; legislation had been thrust down the throats of a recalcitrant Church, and, we are asked to believe, of a no less unwilling House of Commons, while the people at large were seething with indignation at the insults heaped upon the injured Queen and her daughter. By all the laws of nature, morals, and of politics, it would seem, Henry was doomed to the fate of the monarch in the Book of Daniel the Prophet, who did according to his will and exalted and magnified himself above every god.'[4]

If the Pilgrimage of Grace had risen at that moment, when More's firm opposition must have been known throughout the land, what might the consequences have been for Henry? By Pollard's account it was the King, and the King alone who held England just then to the course he had mapped out.

On 23rd March 1534, the Pope finally gave his decision in favour of Katherine of Aragon. This act threw the succession into doubt. Henry replied to it by the Act of Succession of 30th March 1534 which made it treason to oppose the right of succession to Anne Boleyn's offspring, and misprision of treason to speak against it. More's fear about 'oaths' was to be confirmed now, for the act demanded 'that all nobles of the realm, spiritual and temporal, and other subjects arrived at full age, should be obliged to take corporal oath, in the presence of the King or his commissioners, to observe and maintain the whole effect of the act'. Commissioners drew up oaths which broadened the intention of the act in a manner pleasing to the King, by prescribing for the laity an oath concerned with the succession, and for the clergy another denying the supremacy of

Rome and totally rejecting any papal authority in England. Members of both houses of Parliament took the oath on the day the act was passed, though in what form we do not know. Twelve days after, it being Low Sunday, More went from Chelsea to St. Paul's, and then afterward to the house of John Clement, his one-time secretary, who had married Margaret Gigs, the affectionate orphan More adopted. It was not possible then for him to move about unmarked, and his presence in the city was reported to the commissioners, who followed him to Clement's house and served notice upon him to appear next morning before the commissioners at Lambeth Palace to take the new oath. Among the commissioners were three who knew only too well More's views about the divorce and the supremacy—Cranmer, the Archbishop; Audley, the Lord Chancellor; and Thomas Cromwell, Secretary of State.

Roper explains that before More left for Lambeth he did as he was wont to do on every occasion, he got himself to church to be confessed, 'to hear mass and to be houseled'. 'And whereas he used evermore before, at his departure from his house and children (whom he loved tenderly) to have them bring him to his boat, and there to kiss them all, and bid them farewell, then he would suffer none of them forth of the gate to follow him but pulled the wicket after him, and shut them all from him, and with an heavy heart (as by his countenance it appeared) with me, and our four servants, there took his boat towards Lambeth. Wherein sitting still sadly a while, at last he rounded me in the ear and said, "Son Roper, I thank our Lord, the field is won". What he meant thereby then, I wist not. Yet loath to seem ignorant I answered, "Sir, I am thereof very glad". But as I conjectured afterwards it was for that the love he had to God wrought in him so effectually, that it conquered in him all his carnal affections utterly.'

More was never to see his Chelsea home again.

What transpired at Lambeth we know full well for he described it in much detail to Margaret after his committal to the Tower. More was required (by the special malevolence of Anne Boleyn, Roper believed) to take the oath of supremacy, not simply the oath to the succession.

'When I was called before the Lords at Lambeth, I was the first that was called in, albeit, Master Doctor the Vicar of Croydon was come before me, and divers others. After the cause of my sending for, declared unto me (whereof I somewhat marvelled in my mind, considering that they sent for no more temporal men but me) I desired sight of the oath, which they shewed me under the great seal. Then desired I the sight of the act of the Succession, which was delivered me in a printed roll. After which read secretly by myself, and the oath considered with the act, I shewed unto them, that my purpose was not to put any fault either in the act or any man that made it, or in the oath or any man that swear it, nor to condemn the conscience of any man. But as for myself in good faith my conscience so moved me in the matter, that though I would not deny to swear to the succession, yet unto the oath that there was offered me I could not swear, without the jeoparding of my soul to perpetual damnation.'[5] The Lord Chancellor expressed his sorrow at this and warned More of the indignation it would cause the King. More was the first to refuse, he said, and showed him the lengthy roll of those who had already sworn. Nevertheless More still refused and was then sent down into the garden; but the day was hot, and he 'tarryed in the old burned down chamber' and looked down into the garden and watched those who after him were brought in to swear, and servilely complied, as though the supremacy were nothing, and saw how Latimer walked cheerfully about with the other doctors and chaplains to the Archbishop and 'he laughed and took one or twain about the neck so handsomely, that if they had been women, I would have went he had been waxing wanton'. And he saw the Vicar of Croydon strutting very proudly about and, that he might be seen of all, going into the buttery bar of the palace and loudly calling for a drink.

Once again More was examined. And still he refused. Archbishop Cranmer pointed out to him that since he found the whole matter of the oath-taking uncertain, 'and condemned not the conscience of them that swarc', why could he not take the oath knowing that of one thing he must be certain, that it was his bounden duty to obey his sovereign lord the king? 'And therefore are you bounded to leave the doubt of your unsure conscience in refusing the oath, and take the sure way in obeying your prince, and swear it.' The subtlety of this confused and silenced More; he could think of no ready answer. But he replied that this seemed to be one of the cases where he felt compelled to obey his conscience rather than his prince, whatever others thought or did.

The Abbot of Westminster replied that surely he must think his conscience wrong when he saw that the great council of the realm had not been afraid to swear? More answered that he would have reason indeed to doubt his conscience if it had been Parliament on one side and he alone on the other, but he did not feel bound to conform to the Council of one realm against the General Council of Christendom. Thomas Cromwell then swore a great oath and said that he had liever his only son had lost his head than that More should refuse the oath, for now, he hinted, the King would conceive the suspicion that More had contrived the whole business of the nun of Canterbury. (This was pure bullying.)

When the matter of the succession was raised again, More replied that he would be prepared to swear to that if the oath were framed in such a manner that it conformed to his conscience. But that he wanted to make conditions about this, too, was not well received, and in the end More was committed to the Abbot of Westminster to be kept prisoner.

What should be done with him was decided by correspondence between Cranmer and Cromwell, Cromwell writing for the King. Cranmer proposed that More's readiness to swear to the succession should be accepted, and that he should be made to swear, but that exactly what he had sworn to should be kept secret, unless it was to the King's benefit at any time to make it known. Thus it might well be noised abroad that More had sworn, and so the Emperor, the Pope, and all the King's enemies would be confounded. Cromwell was resolute that no effort should be spared to humble More, and so he rejected the compromise. If permission were granted to More to make his own terms then other men would seek to do the same to 'the utter destruction of the King's whole cause, and also to the effect of the law made for the same'. The King, in fact, had gone so far that he could not risk even the rumour of having made concessions to More. Therefore, for his contumacy, More was committed to the Tower. On his way there, his conductor, Sir Richard Cromwell, observing that he was still wearing about his neck the gold chain, as was his custom, advised him to send it home to his wife or children for safe keeping. 'Nay, sir,' said More. 'That I will not. For if I were taken in the field by my enemies, I would they should somewhat fare the better by me.'

Mr. Lieutenant received him at the Tower, and the porter demanded of him his upper garment. 'Mr. Porter,' he said, 'here it is,' and took off his cap and delivered it to him, saying, 'I am very sorry it's no better for you.' 'Nay, sir,' said the Porter, 'I must have your gown.' It was a thin little joke for one so witty, and More's low spirits could not have been raised very high by it.

# CHAPTER TWELVE

# 'GOD MAKETH ME A WANTON'

More was lodged in the lower ward of Bell Tower. The vaulted room is still there; it can hardly have changed much across the centuries, except that of its two arrow slits one has been converted into a window. The other, in a recess, looks down on to the causeway leading to Byward Tower along which the Carthusian fathers must have passed to their martyrdom, watched by Sir Thomas and his daughter Margaret. There is a stove in the room, thickly bricked in, and with an entrance like the mouth of a dovecote. It cannot have given much heat. In the upper ward of the Tower, Fisher was lodged. He had the better room, but he complained bitterly of the cold, the food and the bedding throughout his imprisonment.

Thomas More was permitted his personal servant, John Awood, to wait on him. For their board and lodging he had to pay quite heavily, and it does not appear that they enjoyed very satisfactory fare. Indeed, the Lieutenant of the Tower, Sir Edmund Walsingham, an old friend of Sir Thomas, visited him expressly to apologize, and to say that he would gladly make him more comfortable but for his fear of the wrath of the King. To which More replied characteristically, that he verily believed what Mr. Lieutenant said, and heartily thanked him; 'And assure yourself, Mr. Lieutenant, I do not mislike my cheer; but whensoever I do, then thrust me out of your doors.'

More seems to have done his best to turn this imprisonment into the equivalent of that monastic life for which he had

longed as a young man, and to prepare himself against the
future as though his martyrdom were certain. He did not
neglect his health. Lady Alice, if we are to trust the story related in *Dialogue of Comfort*, found him in a stout chamber with
mats of straw hung upon the walls and placed under foot, so
that he might keep warm. She complained, however, that to
live locked up would frighten her so much that she would die
of loss of breath. At which Sir Thomas smiled to himself, remembering that never at home could she rest in her bed if she
believed the house not tightly locked at door and window.

More corresponded with his beloved Margaret continually;
she was his mouthpiece to his friends, and he managed to write
to her even when deprived of writing materials and forced to
use a piece of charcoal from the stove. His deprivations, though
irksome at the end, cannot have been serious during the major
part of his confinement, for he succeeded in writing two major
works, *The Dialogue of Comfort* and *Treatise on the Passion*, while
in the lower ward of Bell Tower. He was therefore neither an
idle nor an unhopeful man, and his self-discipline was strong
enough to compel him to go on wearing the hair shirt which
his daughter Margaret was accustomed to wash for him. His
liberties in prison seem to have varied from time to time. At
one period he was allowed access to the gardens, but in another
he was closely confined again, for what reason we cannot tell,
though it may well have been in punishment for correspondence with Fisher.

Roper relates that when Sir Thomas had been in the Tower
a month, Margaret, 'longing to see her father, by earnest suit at
length got leave to go to him. At whose coming . . . among
other communication he said unto her, "I believe (Meg) that
they that have put me here, ween they have done me a high
displeasure. But I assure you on my faith, mine own dear
daughter, if it had not been for my wife and you that be my
children, whom I account the chief part of my charge, I would
not have failed, long ere this, to have closed myself in as strait

a room and straiter too. But since I come hither without mine own desert, I trust that God of his goodness will discharge me of my care, and with his gracious help supply my want among you. I find no cause (I thank God, Meg) to reckon myself in worse case here, than in mine own house. For methinketh God maketh me a wanton, and setteth me on his lap and dandleth me." '

One of the worst of his torments was the pressure of his family upon him to make his peace with the King. There is no evidence that they misunderstood his motives; on the contrary, they respected his scruples, but were enraged that so fine a man should be persecuted over what appeared to most a triviality while the time-servers and lickspittles throughout the land made frantic haste to swear and be at peace with the King, and win themselves the earthly rewards they coveted. For some of Margaret's letters to her father on the subject of swearing we can make the excuse that they were probably designed to be shown publicly, perhaps even to Cromwell, in order to secure access to her father. But this cannot be said of all. In August 1534, Lady Alice Alington had a remarkable encounter with the Chancellor, Sir Thomas Audley, and wrote a hasty account of it to Margaret:

'The cause of my writing at this time is to shew you that at my coming home within two hours after, my Lord Chancellor did come at a course at a buck in our park, the which was to my husband a great comfort that it would please him so to do. Then when he had taken his pleasure and killed his deer he went unto Sir Thomas Barmeston to bed, where I was the next day with him at his desire, the which I could not say nay to, for methought he did bid me heartily, and most specially because I would speak to him for my father.

'And when I saw my time, I did desire him as humbly as I could that he would, as I have heard say that he hath been, be still a good lord unto my father. And he said it did appear very well when the matter of the Nun was laid to his charge. And as for this other matter, he marvelled that my father is so obstinate in his own conceit, as that every body went forth with all save only the blind bishop and he. And in good faith, said my Lord, I am very glad that I have no learning but in a few Aesop's fables of the which I shall tell you one. There was a country in the which there were almost none but fools, saving a few which were wise. And they by their wisdom knew, that there should fall a great rain, the which should make them all fools, that should be so fouled or wet therewith. They seeing that, made them caves under the ground till all the rain was past. Then came they forth thinking to make the fools do what they list, and to rule them as they would. But the fools would none of that, but would have the rule themselves for all their craft. And when the wise men saw they could not obtain their purpose, they wished that they had been in the rain and defiled their clothes with them.

'When this tale was told my Lord did laugh very merrily. Then I said to him that for all his merry fable I did put no doubts but that he would be a good lord unto my father when he saw his time. He said, I would not have your father so scrupulous of his conscience. And he told me an other fable of a lion, an ass, and a wolf and of their confession.' We have met this fable already and know the burden of it. In Audley's variation the lion was 'assoiled' because, though he confessed to devouring the other beasts, he was a king and it was his nature so to do. The poor ass which had taken but one straw out of its master's shoe for hunger, and so caused the master to catch cold, was not assoiled, but sent to the bishop for so heinous a crime. The wolf, for his greed, was commanded not to pass more than sixpence a meal. When therefore he saw a cow and her calf, when he was very hungry, he said to himself he would certainly make a meal of them but for the injunctions of his ghostly father. 'Notwithstanding that, my conscience shall judge me. And then if it be so, then shall my conscience be thus, that the cow doth seem to me now but worth a groat, and then

# 'GOD MAKETH ME A WANTON'

if the cow be but worth a groat then is the calf but worth two-pence. So did the wolf eat both the cow and the calf. Now good sister hath not my lord told me two pretty fables? In good faith they please me nothing, nor I wist not what to say for I was abashed of this answer. And I see no better suit than to Almighty God, for he is the comforter of all sorrows, and will not fail to send his comfort to his servants when they have most need. Thus fare ye well mine own good sister.'[1]

Margaret took her sister's letter to show to her father in the Tower, and then wrote Alice a long and faithful account of her discussion with Sir Thomas. She explained that she found him not too well, troubled with his diseases 'both in his breast of old, and his reins [kidneys] now by reason of gravell and stone, and of the cramp also that divers nights grippeth him in his legs'. When they had said the psalms and litany and talked to-gether awhile of the family, Margaret ventured to broach the subject uppermost in her mind. She said that she hoped he might find a way to content the King, to whom he owed so much 'that if you should stiffly refuse to do the thing that were his pleasure, which God not displeased you might do . . . it would be both a great blot in your worship in every wise man's opinion and as myself have heard some say . . . a peril unto your soul also'. She spoke to him then of the letter from Alice, re-marking that it was evidence that he was losing the goodwill of his friends.

Her father, smiling, replied, 'What, mistress Eve, (as I called you when you came first), hath my daughter Alington played the serpent with you, and with a letter set you a work to come tempt your father again, and for the favour that you bear him labour to make him swear against his conscience, and so send him to the devil?' And then, briefly reminding her that he had already told her twice just what the position was, he said he could make no other answer except that he had either to obey his conscience or his King, and he did not see a way of doing both.

184

## 'GOD MAKETH ME A WANTON'

More read Alice's letter most carefully, twice, and answered, 'The first fable of the rain that washed away all their wits that stood abroad when it fell, I have heard ere this: It was a tale told among the King's Council by my Lord Cardinal when his Grace was chancellor, that I cannot lightly forget it. For of truth in times past when variance began to fall between the Emperor and the French King, in such wise that they were likely and did indeed, fall together at war, and that there were in the Council here sometime sundry opinions, in which some were of the mind, that they thought it wisdom that we should sit still and let them alone: but evermore against that way, my Lord used this fable of those wise men, that because they would not be washed with the rain that should make all the people fools, went them self into caves, and hid them under the ground. But when the rain had once made all the remnant fools and that they come out of their caves and would utter their wisdom, the fools agreed together against them, and there all to beat them. And so said his Grace that if we would be so wise that he would sit on peace while the fools fought, they would not fail after, to make peace and agree and fall at length all upon us. I will not dispute upon his Grace's counsel, and I trust we never made war but as reason would. But yet this fable for his part, did in his days help the king and the realm to spend many a fair penny.'

Margaret persists that he ought to seek to conform his conscience to the conscience of others, seeing that he knows what manner of men they are, and since Parliament also has commanded this thing. More makes a gentle and considered reply of which the gist is, that if a law is made in any part of Christendom which some men think does not agree with the law of God, and the matter becomes a debated and debatable issue throughout Christendom, then no man 'is bounded to change his own conscience therein, for any particular law made any where, other than by the general council or by a general faith growen by the working of God universally through all Chris-

tian nations; nor other authority than one of these twain (except special revelation and express commandment of God)....'
In other words, in things doubtful, doubt should be respected, and no man ought to be under compulsion about them. If any pressure is to be brought, it can only come when Christendom has decided the issue. He quoted the conflict between St. Bernard and St. Anselm over the immaculate conception of the Virgin Mary as an instance of the respect which must be accorded to differences of opinion, for these two, he said, which were of such contrary opinions now 'be both twayn holy saints in heaven, and many more that were on either side. Nor neither party was there bounden to change their opinion for the other, nor for any provincial counsel either.'

But when he had said all this, which indeed was no more than a recapitulation of arguments used to the Commissioners who had examined him, as well as to Margaret and his friends, and perhaps in substance put before Henry personally, he added mysteriously that he could not give all the reasons why he refused the oath unless the King personally commanded him. Was there here some echo of that 'secret cause' which he said that His Majesty had showed him as to why the English crown was beholden to the Holy See?

Soon there was nothing more to be said. 'When he saw me sit with this very sad, as I promise you, Sister, my heart was full heavy for the peril of his person, for in faith I fear not his soul, he smiled upon me and said: "How now daughter Margaret? What now mother Eve? Where is your mind now? sit not musing with some serpent in your breast, upon some new persuasion, to offer father Adam the apple yet once again?" "In good faith, Father," quoth I, "I can no further go, but am (as I trow Cresede saith in Chaucer) comen to Dulcarnon, even at my wit's end. For since the example of so many wise men cannot in this matter move you, I see not what to say more, but if I should like to persuade you with the reason that Master Harry Pattenson made. For he met one day one of our men, and when

he had asked where you were, and heard that you were in the
Tower still, he waxed even angry with you and said, "Why?
What aileth him that he will not swear? Wherefore should *he*
stick to swear? I have sworn the oath myself." And so I can in
good faith go now no further neither, after so many wise men
whom ye take for no sample, but if I should say like Mr.
Harry, Why should you refuse to swear, Father? for I have
sworn myself.'

And at his laughter about this, she came to the heart of the
matter. She carried a threat from Thomas Cromwell; Parliament is sitting and may proceed savagely against him at any
moment it wills, if he does not come to heel.

More had counted this cost, too. 'I forgot not in this matter,
the counsel of Christ in the gospel, that ere I should begin to
build this castle for the safeguard of my own soul, I should sit
and reckon what the charge would be. I compted, Margaret,
full surely many a restless night, while my wife slept, and went
that I slept too, what peril was possible for to fall to me, so far
forth that I am sure there can none above.' We can surmise
with what loving, burning apprehension Margaret then gazed
upon him. I hope, she replied, that you do not change your
mind when it is too late. 'Too late, daughter Margaret? I beseech our Lord,' More replied, 'that if ever I make such a
change, it may be too late indeed. For well wot I the change
cannot be good for my soul that change I say that should grow
but by fear.'[2]

Dame Alice joined her supplications to those of Margaret.
She visited him in the Tower and 'at her first coming like a
simple woman, and somewhat worldly too, with this manner
of salutations bluntly saluted him, "What the good year, Mr.
More," quoth she, "I marvel that you, that have always been
hitherunto taken for so wise a man, will now so play the fool
to lie here in this close filthy prison, and be content to be shut
up among mice and rats, when you might be abroad at your
liberty, and with the favour and good will both of the King

and his Council, if you would but do as all the bishops and best learned men of this Realm have done. And seeing you have at Chelsea a right fair house, your library, your books, your gallery, your garden, your orchards, and all other necessaries so handsomely about you, where you might, in the company of me your wife, your children, and household be merry, I muse what a God's name you mean here still thus fondly to tarry." After he had a while quietly heard her, with a cheerful countenance he said unto her, "I pray thee good Mrs. Alice, tell me, tell me one thing." "What is that?" (quoth she). "Is not this house as nigh heaven as mine own?" To whom she, after her accustomed fashion, not liking such talk, answered, "*Tille valle, tille valle.*" "How say you, Mrs. Alice, is it not so?" quoth he. "*Bone Deus, bone Deus*, man, will this gear never be left?" quoth she. "Well then, Mrs. Alice, if it be so, it is very well. For I see no great cause why I should much joy of my gay house, or of anything belonging thereunto, when, if I should but seven years lie buried under the ground, and then arise and come thither again, I should not fail to find some therein that would bid me get out the doors, and tell me that were none of mine. What cause have I then to like such an house as would soon forget his master?" '

We can sympathize with Dame Alice who must have felt that this lawyer's answer was an evasion of the point. But did she, after all, so much misunderstand her husband? In a letter of Christmas 1534 to Henry appealing for his clemency in the matter of Sir Thomas's goods so that his family should not continue to suffer, she said that since More's refusal of the oath 'was not of any malice or obstinate mind, but of such a long continued and deep-rooted scruple, as passeth his power to avoid and put away, it may like your most noble Majesty of your most abundant grace to remit and pardon your most grievous displeasure to the said Sir Thomas and to have tender pity and compassion upon his long distress and great heaviness, and for the tender mercy of God to deliver him out of prison and suffer him quietly to live the remnant of his life with your said poor bedewoman his wife and other of your poor suppliants his children.'³ That is not the letter of a stupid woman, nor even of so worldly a one.

In *Dialogue of Comfort*, More argued out the whole problem of resistance and its consequences. He saw just as clearly as Alice the worldly rewards which the 'great Turk' would readily grant him once he forsook his faith. And the 'great Turk' after all did not ask of him that he should forsake all, but only such parts of the faith as did not stand with 'Mahomet's law'. He could swear, as his friends had advised, and keep his opinions to himself. If he did that he would still be able to make his devotions to Christ, no man hindering him. Yet, argued More, if I capitulate in this, how long before I am asked even greater sacrifices, of a kind I cannot possibly foresee, but which will follow from the first capitulation? Furthermore, what guarantee is there that the 'Turk' will keep his promise in anything even 'that he promiseth you concerning the retaining of your well-beloved worldly wealth, for the pleasure of your body'. There was no surety at all, save to keep firm in one's faith, even though to hold fast to that rock was to place not only one's worldly goods, but one's body in peril.

Might not one, however, in bodily torment, deny one's faith? The question was posed in the *Dialogue of Comfort* in the form of yet another temptation to yield. 'If a man in this persecution should stand still in the confession of his faith, and thereby fall into painful tormentry: he might peradventure hap for the sharpness and bitterness of the pain, to forsake our Saviour even in the midst, and die there with his sin, and so be damned for ever. Whereas by the forsaking of the faith in the beginning betime, and for the time, and in yet not but word neither, keeping it still nevertheless in his heart: a man may save himself from that painful death, and after ask mercy and have it, and live long, and do many good deeds, and be saved as St. Peter was.'

To this time-serving sophistry More answered in wonderful prose: 'That man's reason cousin is like a three-footed stool, so tottering on every side, that whoso sit thereon, may soon take a foul fall. For these are the three feet of this tottering stool, fantastical fear, false faith, false flattering hope.' And in this vein he answered the inducement to do lip-service to what he did not believe in order to save his skin.

More feared that his body might be unable to stand up to what might be demanded of it, and dreaded lest the oath should be forced out of him by torture. He wrote to Master Leder, a virtuous priest, on the 16th January, denying the story that he was too obstinate and wilful to appeal to the King for clemency. No, he answered, he was *afraid* to write, not for reasons of pride, but lest he said anything to stir up the King even more against him. For the rest, he can only answer for his own conscience and 'if ever I should mishap to receive the oath (which I trust our Lord shall never suffer me) ye may reckon sure that it were expressed and extorted by duress and hard handling. For as for all the goods of this world, I thank our Lord I set no much store by than I do by dust. And I trust both that they will use no violent forcible ways, and also that if they would, God would of his grace and the rather a great deal through good folks' prayers give me strength to stand . . . for this I am very sure, that if ever I should swear it, I should swear deadly against my own conscience.'

# CHAPTER THIRTEEN

# 'AS BRIDEGROOMS TO THEIR MARRIAGES'

T he oath administered to More, and refused by him, had only a dubious legality. Parliament, that same which More had opened in 1529, proceeded under pressure of the King to make all legal. It passed the Act of Supremacy in 1534 in which it was enacted 'by the authority of this present Parliament, that the king, our sovereign lord, his heirs and successors, kings of this realm, shall be taken, accepted, and reputed, the only supreme head in earth of the Church of England, called *Anglicana Ecclesia*' not only with all styles, honours and dignities which should go therewith, but with full power 'to visit, repress, redress, reform, order, correct, restrain, and amend all such errors, heresies, abuses, offences, contempts, and enormities, whatsoever they be . . . any usage, custom, foreign law, foreign authority, prescription, or any other thing or things to the contrary hereof notwithstanding'. Henry was to possess, by statute at least, powers over the English Church far beyond those demanded by any Pope, for a Pope was bound by decision of the councils of Christendom, the edicts of his predecessors, as well as by the patristic teachings. Henry was now bound by nothing.

The Act of Treasons made it high treason, as from 1st February 1535, 'maliciously to wish, will, or desire by words or writing, or by craft imagine, invent, practise, or attempt any bodily harm to be done or committed to the king's most royal person, the queen's, or their heirs apparent, or deprive them or any of them of their dignity, title or name of their royal estates, or slanderously and maliciously publish and pronounce, by express writing or words, that the king, our sovereign lord, should be heretic, schismatic, tyrant, infidel. . . .' Acts of Attainder were soon to be passed against Fisher and More because they refused the oath. Even so, if More and Fisher were to be executed for high treason, and the new Acts made plain that this was the King's intention, they were going to be executed for offences committed before the Acts were passed. And all the examinations to which both of them were subject after the passage of the Acts of Supremacy and Treasons were directed to securing from them the admissions necessary to justify their execution.

In More's case, the Commissioners were quite unsuccessful, and had to resort to perjury. The key word of the Act of Treasons was 'maliciously': but if More said nothing, refused comment just as he refused to swear, and could not publish anything even if he so willed, how could he be proved guilty of malicious denial of the supremacy, and so executed? The trial therefore came to resemble modern trials behind the Iron Curtain where those who have to be got out of the way are framed by spurious confessions and the like devices, that a legal cover may be given to their destruction.

Parliament did not like the Bill of Treasons, and resisted it. Originally it was so framed that a chance remark might throw almost anyone in danger. Commons therefore stuck for the insertion of this word 'maliciously' into the Bill, and only then was prepared to swallow it. Yet this very safeguard proved of no consequence to protect More and Fisher.

What was threatened against these two was made ominously plain when, after the passage of the Acts, the fathers of that London Charterhouse where More had lived as a youth were condemned to death for refusal of the oath. We shall speak about them presently. But before their actual martyrdom More was visited in the Tower, on the last day of April 1535, by a

King's Commission. It was headed by Master Secretary Cromwell himself. More was invited to sit with them 'but in no wise would'. Cromwell asked whether More had been acquainted by friends with the new statutes passed by Parliament at its last sitting. More answered that he had, but had taken no particular note of them, since he felt that these were matters he need no longer concern himself with, and his opportunities to talk with people were rare. Cromwell then reminded him of the definition of supremacy in the Act, and said that the King now demanded that More should openly express his opinion of the Act of Supremacy there and then to the King's Commissioners, and declare his own decision about it. More replied that he had long ago made known his mind to the King, and in view of the King's assurances to him, this was a question he had good reason to feel ought never to be asked of him. He had cast all such matters from his mind and would not now dispute either the King's titles or the Pope's, but 'the king's true, faithful subject I am and will be, and daily I pray for him and for all his, and for you all that are of his honourable council, and for all his realm. And otherwise than this I never intend to meddle.'

Refusing to accept this withdrawal, Master Secretary Cromwell rejoined with cajolery. The King was not a prince 'of rigour but of mercy and pity', and even though his subjects might prove at times obstinate, yet when they found themselves ready to be 'conformable and submit themselves' His Grace would show mercy; and he would be happy to see More conform so that he might be abroad again in the world among other men. More replied that he never wished to be abroad in the world again if the price were meddling in the world, that is, if the price were a political one. Political ambitions were given over and his whole study was upon the passion of Christ and his own passage hence.

At this virtual refusal to treat with them, the Commission sent him out of the chamber, and when they recalled him it was to remind him that though he was a prisoner, condemned to life imprisonment, yet he was not by this discharged of obedience to the King, and they asked him whether he believed that the King could demand of him 'such things as are contained in the statutes, and upon like pains as he might upon other men'. More replied that he could say no word against such a proposition. At which they once again assured More that though the King was prepared to be gracious to those who conformed, against those who were obstinate he would allow the law to take its full course, and especially against More whose 'obstinacy' was making 'others so stiff'.

'I do nobody no harm, I say none harm,' was More's passionate reply, 'I think none harm, but wish everybody good. And if this be not enough to keep a man alive, in good faith I long not to live. And I am dying already, and have, since I came here, been divers times in the case that I thought to die within one hour. And I thank Our Lord I was never so sorry for it, but rather sorry when I saw the pang past. And, therefore, my poor body is at the king's pleasure. Would God my death might do him good.'

Were the Commissioners made ashamed? Perhaps, for after one more effort to trap More, the Master Secretary spoke gently to him, and sent him away, with the promise that no advantage would be taken of anything he had said to them, an undertaking made useless by his further declaration that a report would be sent to the King and his pleasure made known.

All this More related in great detail to his daughter Margaret so that she and their friends might understand what was afoot and brace themselves against any disaster which might overtake him.[1]

Four days later Margaret visited her father. It was on the 4th of May, when the Carthusians went to their martyrdom. Roper tells us that 'As Sir Thomas More in the Tower chanced on a time looking out of his window to behold one Mr. Reynolds, a religious, learned and virtuous father of Sion, and

three monks of the Charterhouse for the matter of the supremacy going out of the Tower to execution, he, as one longing in
that journey to have accompanied them, said unto my wife,
then standing there beside him, "Lo, doest thou not see (Meg)
that these blessed fathers be now as cheerful going to their
deaths, as bridegrooms to their marriages? Wherefore thereby
mayest thou see (mine own good daughter) what a difference
there is between such as have in effect spent all their days in a
strait, hard, penitential, and painful life religiously, and such
as have in the world, like worldly wretches, as thy poor father
hath done, consumed all the time in pleasure and ease licenti-
ously. For God, considering their long-continued life in most
sore and grievous penance, will not long suffer them to remain
here in this vale of misery and iniquity, but speedily hence take
them to the fruition of his everlasting deity; whereas thy silly
father (Meg) that, like a most wicked caitiff, hath passed the
whole course of his miserable life most pitifully, God, thinking
him not worthy so soon to come to that eternal felicity, leaveth
him here yet, in the world further to be plunged and turmoiled
with misery.'

The London Carthusians were first accused in the spring of
1534 and their prior and steward imprisoned in the Tower.
They were released upon swearing some kind of oath, with
which their consciences were not offended, but the prior, John
Houghton, warned the brethren that a further attack was
bound to be made, and sought to prepare them for it by days
of fasting and prayer. On the last day of this preparation, when
John Houghton was celebrating Mass, the brothers experienced
a strange presence, 'a soft whisper of air, which some perceived
with their bodily senses, while all experienced its sweet influence upon their hearts', and knew that the Holy Ghost had
descended among them.

If Roper is to be trusted, the Master Secretary came privately
soon after the Tyburn execution of the Carthusians, at the be-
hest of the King, and with many inducements to More to

relent, including tempting promises of the King's favour. This
was the visit which caused More to write with charcoal in his
cell:

> *Eye-flattering Fortune, look thou never so fair*
> *Nor never so pleasantly begin to smile,*
> *As though thou wouldst my ruins all repair*
> *During my life thou shalt not me beguile,*
> *Trust shall I, God, to enter in a while*
> *Thy haven of heaven, sure and uniform,*
> *Ever after thy calm look I for a storm.*

There was a further examination by the persistent Commissioners. In a letter (3rd June 1535) to the beloved Meg, More
with a hint of satire wrote 'Here sat my Lord of Canterbury,
my Lord Chancellor, my Lord of Suffolk, my Lord Wiltshire,
and Master Secretary'. They rehearsed to him the view the
King took of his obstinacy and said that his Grace demanded 'a
plain and terminate answer, whether I thought the statute lawful or not and that I should either knowledge and confess it
lawful that his Highness should be supreme head of the Church
of England, or else utter plainly my malignity'. What followed
for a time was very much a repetition of the earlier discussions
with the Commissioners. They pressed for a plain yea or nay,
and More, quite unbrowbeaten, replied that he had rather lose
his head than offend his conscience. Master Secretary put it
bluntly that the law could compel him to answer one way or
another, and More retorted that he had done nothing against
the statute and 'it were a very hard thing to compel me to say,
either precisely with it against my conscience to the loss of my
soul, or precisely against it to the destruction of my body'.

'To this Master Secretary said, that I had, ere this, when I
was Chancellor, examined heretics, and thieves, and other
malefactors, and gave me great praise above my deserving in
that behalf. And he said, that I then, as he thought, and leastwise
bishops did use to examine heretics, whether they believed the

Pope to be head of the Church, and used to compel them to make precise answer thereto. And why should not then the king since it is a law made here that His Grace is head of the Church here, compel men to answer precisely to the law here, as they did then concerning the Pope.

'I answered and said that I protested that I intended not to defend any part or stand in contention, but I said that there was a difference between those two cases, because at that time, as well here as elsewhere through the corps of Christendom, the Pope's power was recognized for an undoubted thing, which seemeth not like a thing agreed in this realm, and the contrary taken for truth in other realms. Whereunto Master Secretary answered, that they were as well burned for the denying of that, as they be beheaded for the denying of this, and therefore as good reason to compel them to make precise answer to the one as to the other.

'Whereto I answered that since in this case a man is not by law of one realm so bound in his conscience, where there is a law of the whole corps of Christendom to the contrary in matter touching belief, as he is by a law of the whole corps, though there happen to be made in some place a law local to the contrary, the reasonableness or unreasonableness in binding a man to precise answer standeth not in the respect of difference between beheading or burning, but because of the difference in charge of conscience, the difference standeth between heaven and hell.'[2]

Once again the oath was presented to him, and once again he refused to take it. They said to him that he did not seem very sure in his conscience. Why, if he disliked the statute, and would as lief be out of the world as in it, did he not speak out plainly against it? More made an answer of the most remarkable humility: 'As the truth is, that I have not been a man of such holy living as I might be bold to offer myself to death, lest God for my presumption might suffer me to fall, and, therefore, I put not myself forward but draw back. Howbeit if God draw

me to it Himself, then I trust in His great mercy that he shall
not fail to give me grace and strength.'

Cromwell's reply was sour and rough, for Machiavelli's
disciple found Christ's incomprehensible.

John Fisher, the old 'blind bishop' of Rochester, at whom
the Lambeth Commissioners had jeered, a sick, a dying man in
the Tower with More, was suffering the same persecution.
Their 'offences' though not concerted, were linked together in
the King's mind as though they had been, because they were
friends and colleagues whose minds moved in like ways, and
Henry caused the clergy to preach against the 'treasons' of
More and Fisher before More had even been brought to trial.

It is astounding to recall that Fisher was the only English
bishop with the strength to resist the King. He behaved more
like a medieval king-chastening cleric than a sixteenth-century
priest. He had exhibited that strength ever since 1527 when the
divorce proceedings began. As Katherine's confessor and cham-
pion he fearlessly appeared on her behalf before the legatine
court at Blackfriars. He wrote a treatise in her defence, which,
even more than his appearance at Blackfriars, caused him to be
marked down by the King as ripe for destruction. Fisher's
association with Elizabeth Barton, less discreet than that of
More, exposed him to the charge of misprision of treason, and
he escaped worse penalties then by payment of a fine of £300.
When summoned to take the oath of the succession he refused
on the grounds not only of the supremacy but of that part of
the preamble declaring the offspring of Katherine illegitimate.
He was thrown into the Tower, and when the Act of Supremacy was passed was deprived of his see, and charged with
treason. Pope Paul III created him cardinal in this very month
of May 1535 when both More and Fisher were being pressed
to acknowledge the supremacy under penalty of execution.
Henry, in a fury at this act of *lèse-majesté*, declared that if the
cardinal's hat was sent to Fisher, he would be compelled to
wear it on his shoulders, for he would be left no head to put it

JOHN FISHER, BISHOP OF ROCHESTER
By an unknown artist, after Holbein

on; and it was, apparently, immediately after this that More and Fisher received the King's ultimatum—swear, or face Tyburn.

Fisher was tried at Westminster on 17th June, accused of openly declaring 'that the King, our sovereign Lord, is not the supreme head on earth of the Church of England'. It came out at the trial that, under pledge of secrecy, Fisher had at the King's request, asserted 'He believed directly in his conscience, and knew by his learning precisely, that the King was not, nor could be, by the Law of God, Supreme Head in earth of the Church of England'. This considered judgment was given, on the understanding that it was for the King's ears only, to one Richard Rich, the Solicitor-General, a shady little man who played the role in these trials of an informer and provocateur. Fisher pleaded that in all equity, justice, worldly honesty and humanity he could not be accused of maliciously denying the Supremacy when he spoke at the King's request, and for the King's ear alone, to the King's messenger. Rich admitted his purely malevolent intent to extract a confession by any means when he replied to Fisher that, even if he had made such a promise or undertaking as Fisher declared, it was no discharge to him in law. No matter, in other words, how extracted, a confession was a confession.

Fisher was condemned to the Tyburn execution, and might have suffered it if his state of health had not made it uncertain whether he could survive the journey on the hurdle. His sentence therefore was commuted to beheading on Tower Hill. He was awakened early on the morning of 22nd June and told that it was the King's pleasure that he should be executed that day. Fisher's courage was as great as More's. He asked what time it was, and was told that it was about five. 'What time must be mine hour to go out hence?' The Lieutenant replied that he would go out about ten o'clock. 'Well then, I pray you let me sleep an hour or twain. For I may say to you, I slept not much this night—not for fear of death, I tell you, but by reason of great sickness and weakness'. At his execution, this lean, wasted man summoned the strength to ask in a strong voice for the prayers of the crowd. 'Hitherto I have not feared death. Yet I know that I am flesh, and that St. Peter, from fear of death, three times denied his Lord. Wherefore help me, with your prayers, that at the very instant of my death stroke, I faint not in any point of the Catholic faith for any fear.'

A fortnight later More was to follow him to the block, and his head was to replace Fisher's upon London Bridge.

The two imprisoned men had been in communication. Small gifts had been exchanged. Fisher sent More half a custard at one time, and some green sauce at another. More sent Fisher some apples and oranges during the cold weather. John Awood, More's servant, and George Golde, the lieutenant's man, had been the go-betweens, carrying verbal or written messages, of the sort that prisoners exchange to keep their spirits up. When these facts were discovered the servants were interrogated. What emerged was nothing more than that Sir Thomas had told Fisher that he would not dispute the King's title, but (as was the answer so many times) meditate from henceforth only on his going-forth. Fisher had raised with More the significance of the word 'maliciously' in the Act. More replied that this one word would not save them, for everything would depend on the interpretation. When More himself was questioned about these offences against prison discipline, he spoke of his letters to Margaret, but appears to have remained silent about the *Dialogue of Comfort* and other writings in the Tower, a well-kept secret if ever there was one. The *Dialogue* alone would have sufficed for his condemnation.

Nevertheless, though little of value was discovered in these interrogations, the confederacy of More and Fisher formed an important part of More's indictment, as we shall see. When the correspondence was discovered, the Council sent three officials, Mr. Rich, Solicitor-General (and provocateur in Fisher's case), Sir Richard Southwell, and a man named Palmer to seize More's books and writing materials. During the packing of the books a conversation was alleged to have taken place between Rich and More which formed an important part of the indictment. When the books were taken away More closed the shutters of his cell, as though this was the end. The Lieutenant asked him why he had done this, and he replied, with the wit which never deserted him, that as his wares were now all gone, the shop windows might as well be shut.

Aged and feeble, white-haired and bearded from long imprisonment, and scarce able to stand, More was taken to Westminster Hall for trial on 1st July 1535. Fisher was already dead, and the quarters of the martyred Carthusians withering on the gates of London Bridge and Charterhouse. All in the kingdom had sworn, or so it must have seemed to Thomas More; he was left quite alone; the European Christendom he was defending was as silent as it was impotent. He faced a pliable, scornful tribunal of men who had swallowed so many camels to keep their place and power that they could not understand why More should continue to strain at a gnat. Behind them was the fury of a malevolent king who would fall on them as readily as on More should they fail him, and beneath them all a supine, dazed people.

The Commission of Oyer and Terminer, empowered to hear treason against the King, was presided over by Audley, the Lord Chancellor; the Duke of Norfolk was a member, so was Lord Rochfort, brother of Anne Boleyn, and the Earl of Wiltshire, her father. Thus the Boleyn party was strongly represented. The long indictment was based on the Act of Supremacy 26, Hen. VIII, caps. 1 and 13. It hung on three counts, that More had maliciously opposed the King's second marriage, that he had conspired with John Fisher against the Act, and that he had admitted his treasonable views to Richard Rich, the Solicitor-General.

Roper reports the perjury of the plausible Rich and fixes for ever the portrait of the pliant instrument of a tyranny, a type, alas, of which the world is full again.

'Shortly hereupon Mr. Rich (afterwards Lord Rich) then newly appointed the King's solicitor, Sir Richard Southwell, and Mr. Palmer, servant to the Secretary, were sent to Sir Thomas More into the Tower, to fetch away his books from him. And while Sir Richard Southwell and Mr. Palmer were busy in trussing up of his books, Mr. Rich, pretending friendly talk with him, among other things of a set course, as it seemed, said thus unto him: "Forasmuch as it is well known (Mr. More) that you are a man both wise and well learned, as well in the laws of the Realm, as otherwise, I pray you therefore, Sir, let me be so bold as of good will to put unto you this case. Admit there were, Sir," quoth he, "an Act of Parliament, that all the Realm should take me for the King, would not you (Mr. More) take me for the King?" "Yes, Sir," quoth Sir Thomas More, "that would I." "I put the case further" (quoth Mr. Rich) "that there were an Act of Parliament that all the Realm should take me for the Pope, would then not you, Mr. More, take me for the Pope?" "For answer," quoth Sir Thomas More, "to your first case, the Parliament may well (Mr. Rich) meddle with the state of temporal princes; but to make answer to your second case, I will put you this case, Suppose the Parliament would make a law, that God should not be God, would you then, Mr. Rich, say God were not God?" "No, Sir," quoth he, "that would I not, since no Parliament may make any such law." "No more" (said Sir Thomas More, as Mr. Rich reported of him) "could Parliament make the King supreme head of the Church." '

Roper goes on to say that it was upon Rich's evidence solely that Sir Thomas was indicted of treason. That is not so; whether Rich had perjured himself or not More would have been disposed of, just as Fisher had been. But it was useful to the Commission to have something resembling evidence upon which to base their verdict. More's reply, for a sick man, was so confident and damning that once again we are forced to marvel:

' "If I were a man (my Lords) that did not regard an oath, I need not (as it is well known) in this place, at this time, nor in this case to stand as an accused person. And if this oath of yours (Mr. Rich) be true, then pray I that I may never see God in the face, which I would not say, were it otherwise, to win the whole world." Then recited he unto them the discourse of all their communication in the Tower according to the truth, and said, "In faith, Mr. Rich, I am sorrier for your perjury than for mine own peril, and you shall understand that neither I, nor no man else to my knowledge ever took you to be a man of credit as in any matter of importance I, or any other would at any time vouchsafe to communicate with you. And (as you know) of no small while I have been acquainted with you and your conversation, who have known you from your youth hitherto. For we long dwelled both in one parish together, where, as yourself can tell (I am sorry you compel me so to say) you were esteemed very light of tongue, a great dicer, and of not commendable fame. And so in your house at the Temple (where hath been your chief bringing up) were you likewise accounted. Can it therefore seem likely unto your honourable Lordships, that I would, in so weighty a cause, so far overshoot myself, as to trust Mr. Rich (a man of me always reputed for one of so little truth, as your Lordships have heard) so far above my sovereign Lord the King, or any of his noble counsellors, that I would unto him utter the secrets of my conscience touching the King's supremacy, the special point and only mark at my hands so long sought for? A thing which I never did, nor never would, after the Statutes thereof made, reveal it, either to the King's Highness himself, or to any of his honourable councillors, as it is not unknown to your house, at sundry times, and several, sent from his Grace's own person unto the Tower to me for none other purpose. Can this in your judgment (my Lords) seem likely to be true? And if I had done so indeed, my Lords, as Mr. Rich hath sworn, seeing it was spake but in familiar secret talk, nothing affirming, and only in the putting of [hypothetical] cases, without other displeasant circumstances, it cannot be justly taken to be spoken *maliciously*. And where there is no malice there can be no offence." '

Rich called Sir Richard Southwell and Mr. Palmer to swear to the talk that had passed with Sir Thomas in the Tower. They had not heard! They had been too busy 'trussing up Sir Thomas More's books in a sack' to listen to an expression of opinion on a subject all the learned men of England would have given their ears to have heard Sir Thomas More expound. They had paid no attention to the matter for which More's life was forfeit! Mr. Rich earned his promotion to the peerage the hard way.

More, his legal acumen unimpaired by long imprisonment and ill health, then went on to deal with the relevance of the word 'maliciously' in the Act, pointing out that Parliament had inserted this word in order that no one who uttered something without malicious intent should ever find himself as a result in danger of his life. *Malice* must mean, by the Act, *malevolence*. It is necessary to prove malevolent intent. The word *maliciously* was in the Statute for the same reason that the word *forcible* is found in the statute of forcible entries. If a man enter peaceably, there is no offence, and it is the same in the other Act, if a man is without malice in his utterances, then they are not treasonable.

In his reply to the first part of the indictment, malicious opposition to the King's second marriage, More replied, justly, that he had been silent, and 'your statute cannot condemn me to death for such silence, for neither your statute nor any laws in the world punish people except for words and deeds'. To the prosecuting counsel's reply that silence was a sure proof of malice against the statute, as every subject on being asked was compelled to answer categorically, More appealed to common law, that 'he who is silent seems to consent'.

The charge of conspiring with the Bishop of Rochester was easily answered, for since the letters had been burnt, no one could charge him precisely that their contents were malicious, treasonable or conspiratorial. The sole evidence of conspiracy really rested on the charge that John Fisher and Thomas More had both used the phrase about the statute being like a two-edged sword, so that whichever way a man responded to it he would be in trouble, for if he answers one way he will risk his soul, and another way, put his body in jeopardy. More answered the accusation by a common-sense appeal to the similarity of their thought and situation. It is nevertheless probable that Fisher got the phrase from More, though it hardly constituted evidence of treason.

It took the gentlemen of the jury, picked knights, squires and gentlemen from the Tower ward, only a quarter of an hour to bring in a verdict of guilty. Audley began hurriedly to pronounce sentence without waiting for More's reply, and More interrupted him. 'My Lord, when I was toward the law, the manner in such case was to ask the prisoner before judgment, why judgment should not be given against him?'

The confused Audley, who had once boasted that he had little brain, halted his judgment that More might reply. More then said, speaking out at last: 'Seeing that I see ye are determined to condemn me (God knoweth how) I will now in discharge of my conscience speak my mind plainly and freely touching my indictment and your Statute withal.

'And forasmuch as this indictment is grounded upon an Act of Parliament directly repugnant to the laws of God and his holy Church, the supreme government of which, or of any part whereof, may no temporal prince presume by any law to take upon him, as rightfully belonging to the See of Rome, a spiritual pre-eminence by the mouth of our Saviour himself, personally present upon earth, only to St. Peter and his successors, bishops of the same see, by special prerogative granted; it is therefore in law, amongst Christian men insufficient to charge any Christian man.'

Roper speaks of More's appeal to Magna Carta, which guaranteed that the English Church should be free and enjoy

all its rights and liberties, and to the King's oath at his coronation to maintain the faith of the land. He claimed that England
had elected to join the communion of Christendom by the fact
that through Pope Gregory and St. Augustine, 'England first
received the Christian faith, which is a far higher and better
inheritance than any carnal father can leave' for it made us 'the
spiritual children of Christ and the Pope'. And once again, and
for the last time before his judges, when Audley asked him why
he of all the learned stood out against the statute, he appealed
to the Christendom in which he had been nurtured against the
brash young nationalism he was facing. 'If the numbers of
bishops and universities be so material, as your Lordships seemeth to take it, then see I little cause (my Lords) why that thing
in my conscience should make any change. For I nothing
doubt, but that though not in this Realm, yet in Christendom
about they be not the least part, that be of my mind therein.
But if I should speak of those that be already dead (of whom
many be now saints in heaven) I am very sure it is the far
greater part of them, that all the while they lived, thought
in this case that way that I think now. And therefore am I not
bound (my Lords) to conform my conscience to the council of
one realm against the General Council of Christendom.'

This ranging of the whole of Christendom against the realm
of England caused the Duke of Norfolk to burst out, 'Now,
Sir Thomas, you shew your obstinate and malicious mind!'
'Noble Sir,' replied More, 'not any malice or obstinacy causeth
me to say this, but the just necessity of the Cause constraineth
me for the discharge of my conscience, and I call God to witness, no other than this hath moved me hereunto.'

Lord Chancellor Audley, loth to have the sole burden of
judgment upon him, then openly asked the advice of Lord
Fitz-James, the Lord Chief Justice, who was a member of the
commission. He received a lawyer's reply: 'My Lords all, by
St. Julian, I must needs confess, that if the Act of Parliament be
not unlawful, then is not the indictment insufficient.' Thomas

More's great-grandson likened this to the answer of the Scribes and Pharisees to Pilate—'if this man were not a malefactor, we would never have delivered him unto you'. We may imagine that Audley had little inclination to dwell upon the reply. 'Lo, my lords,' he made haste to say, and with obvious relief, 'lo, you hear what my Lord Chief Justice saith,' and so gave judgment that Sir Thomas More 'should be brought back to the Tower of London by the help of William Kingston, Sherriff, and from thence drawn on a hurdle through the City of London to Tyburn, there to be hanged till he be half dead, after that cut down yet alive, his privy parts cut off, his belly ripped, his bowels burnt, and his four quarters set up over the four gates of the City, his head upon London Bridge'.

The Great Turk, whom More had foreseen would stop at nothing to have his will, thus took his revenge. The sentence, however, was not carried out; of his mercy some days later the King gave his pardon and commuted the sentence to beheading. When Sir Thomas More was apprised of this mercy he replied, 'God forbid that the king should use any more such mercy unto any of my friends; and God keep all my posterity from such pardons.'

After the passing of sentence More was once again asked if he had anything more to say in his defence. He replied: 'More have I not to say (my Lords) but like as the blessed Apostle St. Paul, as we read in the Acts of the Apostles, was present, and consented to the death of St. Stephen, and kept their clothes that stoned him to death, and yet be they now both twain holy saints in heaven, and shall continue there friends for ever, so I verily trust and shall therefore right heartily pray, that though your Lordships have now in earth been judges to my condemnation, we may yet hereafter in heaven all meet together to our everlasting salvation.'

More was taken back to the Tower. Sir William Kingston, the Constable, brought him from Westminster to the Old Swan Wharf and tried to comfort him, the tears running down

his cheeks. But it was More who turned comforter, saying,
'Good Mr. Kingston, trouble not yourself, but be of good
cheer. For I will pray you, and my good Lady your wife, that
we may meet in heaven together, where we shall be merry for
ever.'

His son John, Margaret Roper and Margaret Clement
waited at the wharf for their father's blessing. Perhaps Roper
was there, and the maid Dorothy Colley, too. Roper writes not
of himself, but of Margaret, that she, who 'desired to see her
father, whom she thought she should never see in this world
after, and also to have his final blessing, gave attendance about
the Tower Wharf, where she knew he should pass by, ere he
would enter into the Tower. There tarrying for his coming
home, as soon as she saw him, after his blessings on her knees
reverently received, she, hasting towards, without consideration of care of herself, pressing in amongst the midst of the
throng and the Company of the Guard, that with halberds and
bills were round about him, hastily ran to him, and there
openly in the sight of all them embraced and took him about
the neck and kissed him' (not able to say any word, but *Oh my
father, oh my father*), 'who well liking her most daughterly love
and affection towards him, gave her his fatherly blessing, and
many goodly words of comfort besides, from whom after she
was departed, she not satisfied with the former sight of her dear
father, having respect neither to herself, nor to the press of the
people and multitude that were about him, suddenly turned
back again, and ran to him as before, took him about the neck,
and divers times together most lovingly kissed him, and at last
with a full heavy heart was fain to depart from him; the beholding thereof was to many of them that were present so
lamentable, that it made them for very sorrow to mourn and
weep.'

On Monday, 5th July, the day before he went to the scaffold,
Thomas More sent his last letter, not indeed to his wife, Dame
Alice, but to Margaret Roper; he wrote it with a charcoal:

'Our Lord bless you good daughter and your good husband and your little boy and all yours and all my children and all my grandchildren and all our friends. Recommend me when you may to my good daughter Cecily, whom I beseech our Lord to comfort, and I send her my blessing and to all her children and pray her to pray for me. I send her an handkercher and God comfort my good son her husband. My good daughter Dauncey hath the picture in parchment that you delivered me from my Lady Coniars, her name is on the back side. Shew her that I heartily pray her that you may send it in my name to her again for a token from me to pray for me.

'I like special well Dorothy Colley, I pray you be good unto her. I would wit whether this be she that you wrote me of. If not I pray you be good to the other, as you may in her affliction and to my good daughter Joan Alleyn to give her I pray you some kind answer, for she sued hither to me this day to pray you be good to her.

'I cumber you good Margaret much, but I would be sorry, if it should be any longer than tomorrow, for it is St. Thomas's even, and the utas of Saint Peter and therefore tomorrow long I to go to God, it were a day very meet and convenient for me. I never liked your manner toward me better than when you kissed me last for I love when daughterly love and dear charity hath no leisure to look to worldly courtesy.

'Fare well my dear child and pray for me, and I shall for you and all your friends that we may merrily meet in heaven. I thank you for your great cost.

'I send now unto my good daughter Clement her algorism stone and I send her and my good son and all hers God's blessing and mine.

'I pray you at time convenient recommend me to my good son John More. I liked well his natural fashion. Our Lord bless him and his good wife my loving daughter, to whom I pray be good, as he hath great cause, and that if the land of mine come to his hand, he break not my will concerning his sister Dauncey.

## 'AS BRIDEGROOMS TO THEIR MARRIAGES'

And our lord bless Thomas and Austen and all that they shall have.'

The algorism stone must have been a slate which More used after he had been deprived of writing materials in prison. There is no message in this for his wife, though earlier letters had contained them. Was he grieved that she was not at the Old Swan Wharf? Her disapproval of his conduct in plunging the family from eminence and affluence into poverty and disgrace had been made clear enough. In the fatal May she solicited Thomas Cromwell to be allowed to wait upon the King's gracious majesty to plead that her poverty might be relieved, for she had been forced to sell part of her wearing apparel to raise the money, not only to keep the house going, but to pay the '15 shillings for the board-wages of my poor husband, and his servant'. Well, she was not mentioned, and the rest is silence.

On the expected and longed-for morning of the 6th, the eve of the translation of the relics of St. Thomas of Canterbury, that earlier martyr to the wrath of kings, Thomas Pope, More's old and singular friend, came with the message of the King and the Council that he was to die at nine. The humility of More's answer is not feigned:

'Mr. Pope, for your good tidings I most heartily thank you. I have always been bounded much to the King's Highness for the benefits and honours which he hath still from time to time most bountifully heaped upon me, and yet more bounded I am to his Grace for putting me into this place, where I have had convenient time and space to have remembrance of my end, and so help me God most of all, Mr. Pope, am I bound to his Highness, that it pleased him so shortly to rid me of the miseries of this wretched world. And therefore will I not fail most earnestly to pray for his Grace both here, and also in another world.'

'The King's pleasure is further,' quoth Mr. Pope, 'that at your execution you shall not use many words.'

## 'AS BRIDEGROOMS TO THEIR MARRIAGES'

'Mr. Pope' (quoth he) 'you do well that you give me warning of his Grace's pleasure. For otherwise had I purposed at that time somewhat to have spoken, but of no matter wherewith his Grace, or any other should have had cause to be offended. Nevertheless whatsoever I intended I am ready obediently to conform myself to his Grace's commandment. And I beseech you, good Mr. Pope, to be a mean to his Highness, that my daughter Margaret may be present at my burial.' 'The King is well contented already' (quoth Mr. Pope) 'that your wife, children, and other friends shall have free liberty to be present thereat.' One likes to think that there was irony in More's thanks, 'O how much beholden am I to his Grace, that unto my poor burial vouchsafeth to have so gracious consideration'.

The leave-taking brought Thomas Pope to tears, and once again, it was More who turned comforter. Going out to the scaffold he changed into a silk camlet gown sent to him by his faithful friend, the merchant Bonvisi, who had supported him with gifts during his imprisonment. The lieutenant protested that it would go to the executioner, and More was persuaded to change it. Nevertheless, following the example of St. Cyprian, who left his executioner thirty pieces of gold, More sent of what little money was left to him, one angel of gold to the executioner.

We are told that in the sad procession to the scaffold on Tower Hill, More appeared pale and emaciated from his imprisonment. His beard was wild and long and his dress old and coarse. He carried in his hands a red cross and raised his eyes to heaven. As they passed through the crowds a good woman came and offered him a cup of wine, which he refused, saying, 'Christ at his passion drunk no wine, but gall and vinegar'. Alone of More's household, as far as we know, Margaret Clement watched the cortège, that staunch woman who as a little girl had committed tiny faults that she might receive his love with his reproaches. Yet another woman came crying to him concerning the custody given to him of certain papers

211

when he was Lord Chancellor, and he replied grimly, 'Good woman, have patience for one hour's space, and by that time the king's majesty will rid me of the care I have for thy papers and all other matters whatsoever'. And yet a third woman, prompted by his enemies, rumour has said, followed him to accuse him of having done her a great injury by an adverse verdict in the courts. He remembered her case so well, he replied, that 'if he were now to give sentence thereof, he would not alter what he had already done'. Then came a citizen of Winchester, a man sick in his mind, who had come to Sir Thomas for help and counsel when he had been near suicide in past years and, poor unstable man, he cried to Sir Thomas More in his despair, distressed to the point of unbalance at the thought of losing his spiritual father. 'Go and pray for me,' said Sir Thomas, 'and I will carefully pray for you.' History tells us that the man 'went away with confidence, and he never after was troubled'.

We need not doubt these stories, nor that when Sir Thomas came to the scaffold and saw that it was perilous, and even in danger of collapse, he said to the Lieutenant: 'I pray you, Sir, see me safe up, and for my coming down let me shift for myself.'

On the scaffold, he who had intended to have 'spoken somewhat', simply desired the people to pray for him, who died in and for the faith of the holy Catholic Church, asking their prayers for the King, that he might have good counsel, and protesting that 'he died the King's good servant, but God's first'. He kneeled down and said the *Miserere*, then rose up cheerfully, and when the executioner, as the custom was, asked his pardon, he kissed the man and said: 'Thou wilt do me this day greater benefit than ever any mortal man can be able to give me; pluck up thy spirit man, and be not afraid to do thy office; my neck is very short; take heed therefore that thou strike not awry, for saving of thine honesty.'

He covered his eyes himself with a cloth he had brought for

the purpose, then stretched himself on the block, face down-
wards, asking the executioner to wait until he had thrust his
beard aside, saying, it did not deserve to suffer since 'it had
never committed any treason'.

And so he died.

# BIBLIOGRAPHY

To the making of notes there is no end, but how they clutter up a book and impede the reader! I have tried, in this book, to keep them to a minimum. The sources used but to which no notes are appended are:

*The Life of Sir Thomas More*, by William Roper, 1716 edn.
*Utopia*, by Sir Thomas More, the second and revised edition of the translation by Ralph Robinson, 1556.
*Epistles of Erasmus*, from his earliest letters to his fifty-first year, translated with commentary by F. M. Nichols, 2 vols, 1901–4.
*Sir Thomas More*, A Play, edited by Alexander Dyce, Shakespeare Society, London, 1844.
*Chronicles*, Edward Hall, London, 1542.

The context normally indicates the source of quotations in the text.

Other principal sources are these:

*The English Works of Sir Thomas More*, both in Rastell's edition of 1557, and the edition of 1931, Vols. I and II, which reproduces the edition of 1557 with modernized version, and full notes (edited by W. E. Campbell, with notes by various hands).
*The Correspondence of Sir Thomas More*, edited by Elizabeth Frances Rogers, Princeton, 1947 (a most valuable work).
*Life of Sir Thomas More*, by his great-grandson, Cresacre More.

# BIBLIOGRAPHY

*The Life and Death of Sir Thomas More*, by Nicholas Harpsfield, edited by E. V. Hitchcock, notes by R. W. Chambers, 1932.

*Calendar of Letters and Papers of the Reign of Henry VIII* edited by J. S. Brewer (vols. 1–4), J. Gairdner (vols. 5–21), 1862–1910.

*State Papers*, Henry VIII, 1830.

*Henry VIII*, A. F. Pollard, 1902.

*Erasmus of Rotterdam*, J. Huizinga, transl. F. Hopman, 1924.

*Erasmus*, Christopher Hollis, 1933.

*Philomorus, Notes on the Latin Poems of Sir Thomas More*, John Howard Marsden, 1878.

There are many biographies of Thomas More: the two standard and authoritative lives, to which it is obvious that I am myself much indebted, irrespective of specific acknowledgements, are:

*Life and Writings of Blessed Thomas More*, T. E. Bridgett, 1891. (I have used the 1924 edition.)

*Thomas More*, by R. W. Chambers, 1935.

# NOTES

### CHAPTER ONE

1. A. F. Pollard, *Henry VIII*, 1919 edn., p. 438.

### CHAPTER TWO

1. Margaret Hastings, *T.L.S.*, 12th Sept. 1952.
2. *The English Works of Sir Thomas More*, 1931 edn., Vol. I, p. 332.
3. From *A Book about Schools* by A. R. Hope-Moncrieff, 1925, pp. 82–3.
4. *Dialogue of Comfort*, Bk. I, Ch. 13.
5. *Praise of Folly*, trans. W. Kennet, 8th edn.
6. From *The Fruits to be derived from Learning*, 1517, Father Bridgett's translation of the Latin text in *The Life and Writings of Blessed Thomas More*, 1924 edn., p. 13.
7. *Life of Thomas More, Kt.*, by his great-grandson, London, 1726, pp. 15–16.
8. The original poem was in Latin and was included in his *Epigrammata*, the translation is by Archbishop Wrangham. See *Notes on the Latin Poems of Sir Thomas More* by Philomorus (John Howard Marsden), Chap. IV, 1878.

### CHAPTER THREE

1. Burckhardt, *The Civilization of the Renaissance in Italy*, 1944, edn. p. 310.
2. J. A. Symonds, *Renaissance in Italy. Vol. II, Revival of Learning*, 1937, pp. 35–6.
3. Karl Kautsky, *Thomas More and his Utopia*, 1927 edn., transl. H. J. Stenning, pp. 83 et seq.

# NOTES

4. Ibid.
5. Ibid.
6. Ibid.
7. *Praise of Folly*, Bishop Kennet's translation, 8th edn., Preface.
8. Ibid., p. 68.
9. Ibid., pp. 69–70.
10. Ibid., p. 128.
11. *Philomorus*, p. 126.
12. *Apology*, Chap. IX.

## CHAPTER FOUR

1. Kautsky, op. cit., p. 90.
2. *Philomorus*, Kendall's translation, p. 90.
3. Ibid., pp. 59–60.

## CHAPTER SIX

1. *Thomas More and his Utopia*, trans. H. J. Stenning, London, 1927, p. 113.
2. See *Erasmus* by Christopher Hollis, pp. 83 et seq.
3. *English Works of Sir Thomas More*, 1931 edition with modern version by W. E. Campbell, p. 474.
4. Ibid., p. 480.
5. Ibid., p. 491.

## CHAPTER SEVEN

1. *The Correspondence of Thomas More*, ed. Rogers. Princeton, 1947, p. 423.
2. T. E. Bridgett's translation in *The Life and Writings of the Blessed Thomas More*, p. 115.
3. Ibid., p. 131.
4. *Dialogue of Comfort*, Bk. III, Chap. XI.
5. *Dialogue of Comfort*, Bk. II, Intro.

## CHAPTER EIGHT

1. *History of Europe*, p. 514.
2. *The Correspondence of Sir Thomas More*, p. 294.
3. *The Correspondence of Sir Thomas More*, p. 278.

# NOTES

### CHAPTER NINE

1. *Encyclopaedia Britannica*, 14th edn. Article on *Henry VIII*.
2. T. E. Bridgett, *The Life and Writings of Blessed Thomas More*, pp. 245–6.
3. Rastell's translation.

### CHAPTER TEN

1. *The English Works of Sir Thomas More*, 1931, Vol. II, p. 243.
2. *The English Works of Sir Thomas More*, 1931, Vol. II, pp. 215–16.
3. T. E. Bridgett, *The Life and Writings of Blessed Thomas More*, pp. 213–14.

### CHAPTER ELEVEN

1. Buckingham, a descendant of Edward III, and possible claimant to the throne of England, had been executed for treason by Henry in 1521, on negligible evidence, part of which was that he had indirectly consulted a Carthusian brother who had foretold that he should have the crown.
2. *The Correspondence of Sir Thomas More*, pp. 465–6.
3. *The Correspondence of Sir Thomas More*, pp. 498–9.
4. *Henry VIII* by A. F. Pollard, M.A., 1919 edn., p. 306.
5. *The Correspondence of Sir Thomas More*, p. 501.

### CHAPTER TWELVE

1. *The Correspondence of Sir Thomas More*, pp. 511–13.
2. Ibid., pp. 514–32.
3. Ibid., p. 548.

### CHAPTER THIRTEEN

1. *The Correspondence of Sir Thomas More*, p. 553.
2. Ibid., p. 558.

# INDEX

219

# INDEX

# INDEX

More, Alice, 70, 71, 72, 111, 112, 113, 114, 119, 120, 121, 181, 187, 188, 208, 210

    Cecilia, 70, 112, 209

    Cresacre, 37, 38, 113, 116

    Elizabeth, 70, 112, 209

    John (father), 24, 34, 40, 50, 51, 75, 76

    John (son), 70, 112, 208, 209

    Margaret, 37, 70, 111, 112, 115, 116, 117, 173, 176, 180, 181, 182, 184, 185, 186, 187, 194, 196, 200, 208, 211

Morton, Cardinal Archbishop, 31, 32, 33, 34, 35, 41, 76, 95

Mountjoy, Lord, 55, 56, 58

Munday, Sir John, 79

New College, 48

New Inn, 35, 36, 155

Norfolk, Duke of, 93, 114, 142, 144, 171, 201, 206

Oxford Reformers, 45

Pace, Richard, 35

Palmer, Mr., 200, 202, 204

Parnell, 167

Paul III, Pope, 198

Pilgrimage of Grace, 175

*Pitiful Life of King Edward V*, 33

Pollard, 22, 175

Pope, Thomas, 210, 211

Rastell, William, 41, 166

Rich, Father, 168, 169, 170

    Richard, 199, 200, 201, 202, 203, 204

Risby, Father, 169, 170

Robinson, Ralph, 94

Rochfort, Lord, 157, 201

Roper, William, 31, 33, 36, 37, 69, 74, 85, 91, 92, 110, 111, 112, 114, 115, 116, 117, 118, 121, 129, 131, 133, 144, 151, 155, 156, 167, 170, 171, 173, 176, 177, 181, 194, 195, 201, 202, 205, 208

'Ross, William', 162

Sampson, Dr. Richard, 85, 157

Sandys, Lord, 135

*Satyricon, The*, 48

*Sir Thomas More*, 55, 79, 83

Southwell, Sir Richard, 200, 202, 204

St. Anthony's Hospital, 26, 27, 28

Stapleton, 35

Statute of Praemunire, 21, 147, 172

Stow, John, 27

Suffolk, Duke of, 140, 142, 144, 196

*Supplication of Souls*, 159

Surrey, Earl of, 122

Temse, 150

*These Fowre Things*, 40, 41

*Treatise on the Passion*, 106, 181

Tunstall, Dr. Cuthbert, 85, 135, 137, 152, 158, 159

Tyler, Mr., 74

Tyndale, William, 67, 156, 158, 159, 160, 161

*Utopia*, 31, 32, 36, 46, 50, 81, 83, 85, 86, 88, 94–106, 110, 127, 130, 165

Vicar of Croydon, 94, 177

Vaughan, Mr., 167

Vaughan, Mrs., 167

Walsingham, Sir Edward, 180

# INDEX